Every Dog's Survival Guide to Living with a Neurotic Owner

Every Dog's Survival Guide to Living with a Neurotic Owner

Steve Duno

**BARNES
&NOBLE
BOOKS**
NEW YORK

2003 Barnes & Noble Books

ISBN 0-7607-3876-9

Text design by Leah Lococo

Illustrations by Paul Hoffman

Printed and bound in the United States of America

03 04 05 06 07 08 09 M 9 8 7 6 5 4 3 2 1

BVG

Contents

PART 3
The Right Way to Run the Home Environment

INTRODUCTION

LET ME INTRODUCE
MYSELF, "GABBY DEAREST"

W elcome, dogs. Let me introduce myself. I'm Gabby, top-notch advisor to troubled pooches everywhere. Have you got problems? Owner screwing up again? Neighbor's cat just out of reach? New mail carrier a bit too quick with the pepper spray? Worry not, my furry friends; Gabby's here to save the day!

I've led a long life, mates. From the docks of Brooklyn to the show rings of San Francisco, I've seen and done it all. Through good owners and bad, this dog's learned a lot along the way. Now I'd like to share my knowledge with you, in hopes that, by doing so, I'll make life with humans a bit more enjoyable in the days to come.

If there is one thing I have learned, it's that very few dogs are bad to the bone. Sure, some of us are high-strung, bossy, or a little messy, while others are shrinking violets, or a tad on the suspicious side. That's normal. After all, dogs have personalities too, just like people. But very few of us are by nature mean-spirited, spiteful, or out-and-out dangerous.

Most bad dogs aren't born; they are made. When one of

us screws up, it's almost always because an owner has either inadvertently taught us to do so, or else simply hasn't taught us anything at all. When owners don't teach us what they consider to be acceptable behavior, we take it upon ourselves to do what we think we need to do, in order to be safe and happy. All of you know that. But guess what? They don't. It's not their fault—they're two-foots. Remember: To err is human, to forgive, canine.

In this book, I have collected some of what I think are the most telling letters written to me by my canine public, letters which point out the most common mistakes made by neurotic, misguided dog owners. I have arranged them into sections entitled:

1. *New Owner Errors*
2. *Tales of Trouble: Training Mistakes*
3. *The Right Way to Run the Home Environment*
4. *Our Beloved Owners: Can't Live with 'Em, Can't Live without 'Em*

Within these four sections, I cover fifty separate entries, designed to do the following:

◆ define owner mistakes and the problems they cause
◆ explain why the mistakes make us behave so strangely
◆ offer alternative owner actions, and solutions for the immediate problems at hand.

Here's what I want each of you distressed dogs out there to do: First, read through all fifty entries, and see if any of them apply to your situation. If some do, perhaps the advice I give will help explain why your owners are so clueless. Second, I want you to *leave the book in a place where your owner can find it,* so that he or she might discover the awful truth—that most canine misbehaviors are the fault of the owner! Hopefully, he or she will learn how to solve the problem or problems that exist, all by reading my sage advice. If all goes well, life at the old homestead will get better for you, and for the two-foots. Promise!

Oh—one more thing: Don't let on that you can read and write. It would blow their minds.

So, without further delay, let's get on to Part One, *New Owner Errors.* Soon, you will better understand how to deal with your quirky yet loveable two-legged benefactor!

New Owner Errors

D ogs and humans sure have a lot in common. We both form packs, and show great loyalty to our loved ones. We both protect our turf, learn quickly, and have a history of being great hunters (though the closest we get to hunting these days is chasing that crafty squirrel in the park). Because we have so much in common, it's natural that we would come together and keep each other company. They feed and house us, we love and entertain them. Good deal, if you ask me.

Unfortunately, as many of you dogs have found out, many rookie owners don't seem to know the first thing about us. They take us into their homes and hearts, and for that I thank them. But once a new owner gets one of us home, he or she often makes a heap of mistakes that lead to us "misbehaving."

Part One addresses mistakes made by these well-meaning rookies, whose inexperience often leads to conflict between themselves and their new pooches. The twelve letters I have chosen to include here deal directly with the most common errors, so let's get right to them!

Why Dogs Make the Best Pets (For Some)

Dear Gabby,

Help! I am a two-year-old pointer mix who just might be the loneliest, most frustrated dog in the world. Last month, the nicest lady came into the shelter and adopted me. A real sweetheart, she has a small apartment in the city, lives alone, and is gone most of the day. Now Gabby, I don't have to tell you what it's like for a high-energy dog like me to have to mope around this little place all day, waiting for her to show up. When she finally does come home in the evening, she gets mad at me for having rearranged the furniture, or for going potty in her closet. Yesterday, I found some perfectly good chow that she had just thrown away. When she came home and found me eating it in the kitchen, she just about blew her top.

Gabby, I am going stir crazy. I need to get out and play, but she's always too tired at night to take me to the park. I can't keep my legs crossed all day, either; it's beginning to get pretty rank in here. She's a nice person and all, but I'm beginning to think that the shelter was more fun than this prison. What can I do?

Your loyal fan,

Lonely in Las Vegas

DEAR LONELY,

You poor kid! This is a classic case of a human having no concept of what it takes to be a responsible owner. That's not to say that she isn't a great person with great intentions, but only that she's a bit clueless about how much time and effort it really takes to care for one of us (especially one as lively as yourself). Some people fall in love with the idea of having a dog, but have no concept of just how much work it really is until they get one of us pooches home.

Let's look at your case. First, being a pointer mix, you definitely have lots of energy, and need to release it on a regular basis. Dogs bred for hunting are high-strung athletes in need of regular exercise; being cooped up inside an apartment all day is torture for a dog like you, and will inevitably result in some unfortunate behaviors, and in high levels of stress for everyone.

Second, all dogs need companionship on a regular basis. We are, after all, pack animals, bred to crave a group dynamic. To leave one of us alone all day is cruel, to say the least. Do we have whiskers and cry "meow"? I think not. A dog left alone will get stressed and bored, and ultimately get into something it's not supposed to, like the garbage (love it), or the closet (filled with all those yummy shoes).

Third, it is nearly impossible for any dog to go nine or ten hours straight without a potty break. The magical pooch who can actually go that long might eventually develop kidney or bladder problems because of it. Odds are, though, that even the best of us will eventually have an accident somewhere in the home. When the owner gets home and finds the unexpected gift, all bets are off.

In your case, Lonely, your well-meaning owner would be better off with one of those antisocial meow machines, as they tend to get along just fine by themselves for long periods of time. They also have the luxury of a litter box, allowing them to go potty whenever necessary (though personally I think the whole concept is a dirty abomination). She could even make do with a guinea pig or hamster, or a fish tank filled with guppies. But, with her work load, taking on ownership of a complicated, socially dependent creature like you just isn't doable.

If she cannot find a good home for you (one with a nice yard, and people to interact with), she's going to need to hire a pet-sitting service to come over at least once each day to walk and play with you, and to let you have a potty break. She could even have a neighbor take on the responsibilities, or come home herself for an hour at lunchtime.

I know you love her, kid, but you're a dog, not a philodendron. You have needs, and she needs to meet them, or else find someone who can.

Finding the Right Owner

Dear Gabby,

I'm writing you from my cozy kennel here at the local pet shelter. A four-month-old retriever/shepherd mix, I like all the dog company here, but am hoping to find a good home soon.

Lots of people come in to check us out; some are big and loud, others small and quiet. Many have kids, though a few who come in alone are old and slow. They all seem sweet and sincere about wanting me. Gabby, who's best for me to go home with?

Your pal,

Puzzled in Peoria

DEAR PUZZLED,

Ah yes, an embarrassment of riches. Life is good when you're four months old, aye? Everyone, and I mean everyone, loves you. You're a cute, cuddly little fur ball, with soft fur and tiny little teeth. Even your breath is a pleasure. Who wouldn't want to scoop you up?

It's good that you wrote, Puzzled. We want to make sure you go to the best owner, right? Properly matching a dog to the right owner is a crucial ingredient in ensuring a long, happy partnership, so let's talk about that for a bit.

Dogs come in all shapes, sizes, and temperaments. So do people. The trick is to match them up so that they complement each other nicely. Take a frisky, ten-month-old border collie and send her home with an eighty-five-year-old widow with a walker, and you've got a disaster in the making. That little ball of energy will run rings around the frail lady. She won't be able to properly exercise the pooch, or keep up with its intellectual needs (border collies are smart, and need constant challenges). A more docile, manageable breed such as a Maltese or a toy spaniel would be more appropriate in her case, as would an older mixed breed in need of a quiet, laid-back home. Likewise, a passive, fragile breed such as a Maltese would never work for a home filled with kids and lots of activity, as it might become overwhelmed and frightened. For this situation, a more gregarious, resilient, athletic breed (like yourself) would do much better.

The following are some general rules that should be followed when choosing an owner. Though exceptions always abound, dogs who abide by these guidelines will generally do okay:

- If you are an active, robust, gregarious dog of good size (or the potential for it), consider going to a home with a fenced yard, and owners of competent physical ability. Kids are a plus (provided they aren't teasers, hitters, or tail-pullers), as they will help you release pent-up energy. Make sure they are willing to exercise and train you, though, as a dog like you needs guidance, and an outlet for all that liveliness. Hunting and herding breeds fit into this category, as do most of the larger breeds.

- If you are a dog with a more demure, guarded personality, or one who has trouble dealing with lots of chaotic activity, think about going with a person who has a quieter home, one without kids or lots of unpredictable activity. Be sure that the person isn't a complete wallflower, though, as you will need some confidence building in order lead a happy life. Consistency and calmness should prevail. Make sure he or she doesn't baby you too much, and ask to be obedience trained as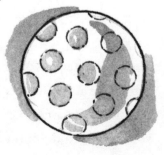

soon as possible. Toy breeds, sighthounds, and dogs with shy personalities fit into this category.

◆ If you are a calm, docile little lap dog type, an older owner might just be the ticket for you. Often they are retired, and have lots of quality time on their hands. Just be sure they are active enough to be able to walk you, and take care of your everyday needs. Most toy breeds fit into this category, as do some terriers, such as the Yorkshire terrier, or the Soft-coated Wheaton. If you were an active little dog like a Jack Russell, pug, or miniature pinscher, though, you should look for a more dynamic home, with active, energetic owners.

◆ Generally, puppies should go with families with at least one or two persons available at all times. When we are young, we need to eat and go potty often, and tend to require constant observation until we are housebroken and trained. Don't go home with a single owner who works all day, as you won't get the care and attention you need.

◆ Older dogs should avoid the hectic atmosphere of a home with kids, and instead go home with a senior citizen with previous dog experience. You are probably already housebroken and trained, making the move that much easier for everyone.

◆ If you are a highly territorial, protective breed such as a Rottweiler, pit bull, mastiff, German shepherd, Akita,

Doberman, chow chow, Chinese shar-pei, or Bouvier des Flandres, look for a highly confident, physically fit owner who has experience working with dominant breeds. He or she should enroll you in obedience class as soon as possible, and socialize you with other people and dogs from an early age. Never go home with a shy, physically challenged person with poor leadership skills, and avoid families with small children, as they might annoy you and cause you to get a bit bossy or nippy.

Good luck, and remember to look extra cute and really sweet when you see that active-looking young couple with well-behaved kids!

Why You Should Hate Pet Shops

Dear Gabby,

I'm writing you for some advice about my health. Though I am only five months old, my hips hurt me, and patches of my fur are falling out. The other puppies in the pet shop don't seem to be much better off, either. Some of us shake uncontrollably, while others growl all of the time, for no reason. We get fed well, though, and the employees here do a good job, and seem to care. Lots of customers come into the shop, and quite a few puppies have been sold in the last few weeks, even though none seemed very healthy or happy. Gabby, do you think there is some kind of mysterious illness affecting us here?

Your admirer,

Achy in Albuquerque

DEAR ACHY,

You've really touched on one of my sore points. Mention "pet shop" to me and I lose it. Though most pet shop owners are well intentioned, the puppies they sell often come from large commercial breeding facilities known as "puppy mills," where breeding bitches are forced to produce litter after litter, year after year, until exhausted, or dead. The caliber of breeding stock used is often very low at these puppy factories; quantity, not quality, is the prime motivator here.

Also, the environment in which the parents and puppies are kept is often dismal. These dirty, dank places almost always lack any standards of cleanliness, and rarely provide the pups with decent social interaction. No cut against you, Achy, but puppies from these doggy dungeons are usually poor specimens destined to suffer permanent physical and emotional problems.

Puppy mills sell their stock to pet shops all over the country, who then display the poor pooches for all the world to see. Who can resist cute little babies in a display case filled with shredded newspaper and squeeze toys?

Pet shops offer cut-rate prices, too, compared to private breeders. Families strolling through a mall see the cuties in the window and can't resist the impulse to take one home at a "bargain." Within a few days, though, many of them regret it.

Hip dysplasia, infectious and immunodeficiency

diseases, skin, coat, and joint disorders, and eye or ear infections are just some of the physiological problems these poor pet shop pooches often suffer from. In addition, profound psychological disorders such as fear aggression, poor hygiene, separation anxiety, profound antisocial behavior, or chronic nervousness are commonplace among these pups, whose first few weeks are spent not in a nurturing, loving environment, but in a crowded, dirty breeding factory, devoid of normal canine interaction.

Achy, your hips may be hurting because of hip dysplasia, or because you haven't been getting the right kind of food and exercise. Also, when fur falls out in clumps, it can mean a poor diet, dermatitis, an allergic reaction, or even abnormally high levels of stress, which pet shop puppies suffer from terribly, from birth.

The best bet for you, my friend, is to find a caring owner willing to spend some money at the veterinarian's office, to diagnose and treat your medical problems. Then, you have to help spread the word to pet shop owners everywhere to stop buying puppies from those awful puppy mills! It's a difficult situation; we want puppies now in the pet shops to find decent homes, yet we also don't want to encourage future sales of poor-quality pets. I think pet shops should sell or adopt

out homeless pets in good health, instead of creating a market for sickly, miserable puppies.

In my opinion, breeding should be left to the experts. By finding a good breeder and spending a little extra money, owners will get healthy pets, while helping to keep the breeds healthy and sound. Spread the word, Achy, and good luck.

When the Owner Brings Home Littermates

Dear Gabby,

My brother and I are three-month-old male beagle pups, from the same litter. Right now we are still with Mom, at the breeder's. But, come this Saturday, we are going home with a nice family. They can't bear to see us split up, so they are taking us both.

Gabby, here's the problem: My snotty brother is on the pushy side, and I'm not too sure I want to share this family with him. Is that selfish of me? Shouldn't I be happy that he and I will be together?

Yours truly,
Romulus in Redondo

DEAR ROMULUS,

That whole "brother's keeper" thing is overrated. I had a littermate bro who used to hog all the milk, and chomp on my ears while I slept. A real son of a bitch. Thankfully, we went our separate ways. Last I heard, he was dumpster diving in Jersey.

Owners make a big mistake when they bring littermates home. Here's why:

First, the bonds formed between littermates often become closer and stronger than those formed with the owner(s), causing a shift in pack loyalties. In effect, the siblings often ignore the authority of the humans, and simply do whatever they choose to do. Two ten-month-old husky littermates, for example, if running together in the park, will blow off their owner's pleas to "Come," in favor of doing their own thing. Among most dogs, it's usually family first.

Second, for those owners bringing home littermates of the same gender, dominance problems can and often do arise. Dogs of the same sex typically try to outdo each other. When two male (or two female) pups from the same litter live together, they are likely to compete—maybe even fight—over who gets what, whether it's social rank, special privileges, territory, or anything else they both take a fancy to. Here's my advice: Owners who want more than one dog should get pups of the opposite sex. They're practically guaranteed to get along better.

Third, having two puppies in the home at the same time makes housebreaking and training doubly hard. While one little home wrecker is a handful, two are near impossible. Why go there? And, if one happens to pick up a bad habit, it's a sure bet that the other will quickly mimic it, and drive the owner batty.

That said, the best way for an owner to successfully keep multiple dogs in a home is to properly raise and train one first. Once it has matured and exhibits excellent obedience, then another puppy can be brought into the picture. The new tyke will have a well-behaved, dominant adult dog to model his behavior after, making the owner's job easier. When the established dog goes potty, for example, the pup will quickly learn to mimic the behavior, at the desired time and place. The age difference will also minimize conflicts between them.

Romulus, see if you can sour your new owners on the idea of taking home your pushy bro. Maybe you can sucker him into growling at you in front of them. Don't worry; someone will give the assertive punk a good home, all to himself. Then, both of you will get to be the top dogs!

Gender Benders

Dear Gabby,

I'm a six-year-old male cocker spaniel with a problem. For the last six years, I've had the run of the home here. No other dogs, cats, ferrets, goldfish—just me and my owners. Perfect.

Then, last week, my owners bring home a new dog! What am I, chopped liver? Do they and the vet know something I don't?

Don't get me wrong, Gabby—I like other dogs, and have plenty of friends at the park. But the one they brought home is a big, burly, pushy male mutt, who thinks it's his job to eat from my bowl, pee on all my spots, and steal chew toys from me when I'm not looking. He might be bigger than me, Gabby, but I've learned a few tricks along the way, and may just have to put "junior" in his place. What should I do?

Yours truly,

Ticked in Toledo

DEAR TICKED,

Peace, brother! Let's not hurt anybody, okay? You've fallen victim to the frailties of the fickle human heart. Your owners probably got it into their heads that you needed company during the day, and decided to get a new buddy for you before you got too old to enjoy the camaraderie. Unfortunately, they brought home a big, untrained male instead of a less-challenging female, or at the very least a puppy of either sex. They aren't aware of the innate power struggles that go on between dogs of the same gender, especially in the beginning of the relationship.

In your case, you have ruled the roost now for six years, only to have your dominion suddenly challenged by this big, pushy doofus. It's not only the presence of the new dog, though; it's the fact that you are both of the same gender. Males instinctively feel the need to vie with other males for control, as do females with other females. It's just the nature of the play, baby.

Owners who bring home a new dog of the same gender as the established animal often spark immediate dominance problems between the two. Same-sex posturing is a common behavior amongst dogs: If two males (or two females) of similar age are in the same home, odds are they will from time to time disagree over issues of possession, territory, rank, privilege, or whatever else both decide to equally covet.

The trick to having two dogs in the home is to vary

their genders and ages. In your case, having to interact with a five-month-old female would be much less stressful and taxing than dealing with this new upstart, whom you see as a direct challenge to your dominance.

When getting more than one dog, owners should always opt for a male and a female, as, at least among canines, opposite sexes get along better. There is just less posturing and competition. They should also bring home a dog who is young enough to not be an immediate threat to the established dog's place as top dog. You wouldn't have felt nearly as threatened by a little puppy, regardless of the gender, right?

If a dog of the same gender has already been decided upon, it should be a juvenile, and preferably neutered, to minimize dominance issues. Though the little pup will eventually grow up and vie for a higher-status position in the pack, the established dog will have years to become accustomed to the newbie, and to the idea of sharing power and control.

In your case, Ticked, the two of you will just have to work out your dominance issues as dogs in the wild have had to do for eons. There will be conflict, but hopefully one of you will come out on top with a minimum of fuss. Let your owners know, however, that they need to let the two of you work it out amongst yourselves. They should not scold you, for instance, if you growl at the new guy for trying to eat from your bowl. It's your right to do that, and it teaches him to respect your space and possessions. Only if a real fight breaks out should they interfere and break it up (with great care—preferably with a hose, bucket of water, or a loud distraction like a big book slammed onto the ground).

Once one of you becomes the clear dominant dog, your owners need to support that status by letting the dominant dog discipline the submissive dog when necessary, as long as it doesn't become too violent. They should pet the dominant dog first, feed him first, and let him go through doors first. That way, they keep the dominance hierarchy intact.

One more thing; make sure your owners get that unruly guy trained as soon as possible. By doing so, they will make it easier to have the two of you together in a controlled manner. Otherwise, he'll jump all over you all of the time, and create major conflict.

Good luck, Ticked. And remember, given a fair chance, he might just turn out to be the best friend you ever had!

What Puppies Prefer: Paper or Crates?

Dear Gabby,

I'm a twelve-week-old shepherd mix, and I'm confused by my owner's housetraining demands. We live in a two-bedroom apartment with no yard, and, most of the time, he has me go potty in the kitchen! Isn't going inside supposed to be a big no-no? Who wants to poop where you eat? Anyway, he puts down the *Post*, and has me go on top of it. Sometimes he leaves me for hours, and that gated kitchen gets pretty stinky. When I went on top of his opened copy of *Esquire* this morning, he hit the roof. The carpet got stained, and I got ragged out. What am I doing wrong?

Yours, confused,

Stinky in Seattle

DEAR STINKY,

Ask your owner how much he'd like doing his business in the kitchen, and then staying in there for a few hours while it funks up the room. He's got his nice little flushy toilet thingy to go in, and what have you got? The *Post?* How barbaric.

Humans have been using the "paper-training" method on puppies for years. Well, I'm here to tell you and everyone else that, as a method, it stinks. Let's talk about why.

A puppy has no concept of what being housebroken means, as his mother took care of cleanup while he was a baby. It's up to the owner to teach him the concept. Many owners attempt to paper-train their puppies in the home; this method works poorly, and only encourages the puppy to eliminate inside the home. Puppies like you end up thinking that going potty indoors is okay, when it isn't. When a pup misses the paper or goes elsewhere in the home (like atop a magazine, or pile of dirty laundry), it gets yelled at, or even struck. What better way to ensure that housebreaking will take ages to occur?

The solution to your problem, Stinky, is to get your owner to abandon the *Post,* in favor of a sturdy plastic travel crate. Let me explain.

All dogs want to keep their sleeping areas clean. It's just canine instinct. Your owner can take advantage of this, and use it to housebreak you. To do so, have him purchase a plastic travel crate, available at any good pet store. While he is not able to directly supervise you, he *must* keep you in this crate. While inside this cozy area, you will instinctively hold off on urinating or defecating.

You should also sleep in the crate, and be in it whenever he cannot be at home with you. And, if he is gone for more than a few hours each day, he'll need to have someone come over and let you out of the crate, to eliminate, eat, or play.

When he's home, the two of you should stay physically close. You shouldn't be able to disappear into unoccupied portions of the home. Your owner should clip a leash onto your collar and tie the other end to his belt loop; you'll have little choice but to follow him around. He'll be able to watch you, and nurture a lasting bond. When you start sniffing around or making quick little circles, he'll know to take you out.

The crate should be appropriately sized to your body. If too big, you'll crawl to the back of it, do your business, then hang out up front, away from the mess. By utilizing a properly sized crate, that won't happen. Your instincts to keep your resting place clean will kick in, and encourage you to hold it.

A properly sized crate should be large enough for a dog to stand up and turn around in. For a puppy, the

owner may have to purchase a small crate for the first four months, and then a larger one later on, to accommodate the pup's growth. Or, he can buy a larger crate, and then place something (like a milk crate) in the back, to take up space. Doing so will save him the expense of buying two crates.

Many owners think we dogs don't like to be in small enclosures. That's their own prejudices talking. You know that dogs love being inside cozy little spaces; it's just part of our "denning" instinct. That's why so many dogs love to crawl beneath a bed or table and hang out. Let him know that the crate is fine by going in there and falling asleep. You can even have him feed you dinner and treats in there, to make it more appealing.

To help ensure good housetraining, have him try these additional suggestions:

- Feed you at regular times, to ensure elimination on a predictable schedule as well.
- Have him take you out to eliminate first thing in the morning. Let him feed you, then insist he take you out again. Puppies often have the need to go right after eating, so get into this habit to ensure success.
- Make sure he takes you out after every meal, and right before you go to sleep.
- Puppies under four months should be taken out every hour on the hour, to build routine, and to prevent accidents. Gradually, this duration can be lengthened.

◆ Be sure he lets you eliminate right after playing, as the excitement will often stimulate your need to go.

If you have an accident in the home, and he has witnessed it, he should clip your leash on you, bring you to the accident, then *firmly scold the mess,* and not you. Sounds goofy? Maybe. The idea behind it is to let you know that feces or urine are unwanted in the home. If he scolds you, you might think that the *act of eliminating* is bad, causing you to become stressed or secretive whenever the need arises. After he scolds the mess, he should bring you to a proper location and allow you to eliminate there, if necessary.

If he takes you out and you do not go, he should bring you back inside and put you in the crate, or else tie your leash to his belt loop. After fifteen minutes, he should take you out again. Eventually, you will go, at which time he should praise you.

After following these instructions for a month, he should be able to slowly give you more and more freedom to roam the home. If at any time you have an accident, however, he should go back to the crate and/or the leash-on-the-belt-loop technique, and start again. Once you can go six weeks without an accident, you'll be housebroken.

One more point: If you have an accident while he is away, tell him to use the same technique described before. He should put your leash on, take you to the mess, *scold the mess,* then take you outside. He shouldn't stick your nose in it, or hit you. Then tell him to clean the mess up thoroughly, using an odor-neutralizing cleaner, available at all pet stores. If the site has any scent remaining, you will home in on it and use it again. Don't hang around while he cleans it up, however, as you might get the idea that it's okay to play with it. A scary, silly thought, but you pups are, well, a little silly for the first year or so.

Puppy Education:
Sign Up Early!

Dear Gabby,

I'm a six-month-old female Australian cattle dog. Last week, we went to the park to meet friends and have a good old time of it. But when my owner and I got there, instead of seeing the gang cavorting wildly, I saw them *sitting, lying down, and coming on command!* I felt like a grifter at a Mensa convention.

Now, whenever I go to the park, the other owners treat me like I'm a thieving dingo. Even my dog buds are starting to ignore me. What's going on?

Yours seriously,

Spurned in Spokane

DEAR SPURNED,

Girl, it's all about higher education these days. Without that diploma, you ain't going nowhere! Seriously, your owner needs to smell the coffee and get the two of you into a local basic obedience class as soon as possible.

You are entering doggy adolescence, my dear, a time that can be very hard for you and your owner to cope with without some behavioral safeguards in place. The other dogs and owners at the park seem to know this now, and have begun some type of obedience training. It's an admirable goal not only for them, but for their owners, who are aware of the need for their dogs to have guidelines taught to them from early on. Both owners and dogs are being responsible enough to work on the training at the park, where distractions make the lessons more challenging.

Unfortunately, your owner hasn't yet made the decision to train you yet, either on his own, or through a respected local training facility. That's a shame, because a smart herding breed like yourself must be craving some direction right about now, true? Admit it; the drills, tricks, and neat behaviors your buds are learning look tempting, don't they?

You'd love being trained! Do you know that your breed is still used to herd cattle in the Australian outback? Think a dummy can do that? Not! It takes a smart pooch to take on such a responsibility. You could learn basic obedience skills in a snap, girl.

My advice to you is to get that lazy owner of yours to sign both of you up for a basic obedience course, as soon as possible. The typical course lasts from six to twelve sessions, and includes all of the crucial training, plus lots of socialization with other dogs and persons. At the very least, you'll learn how to sit, lie down, stay, come, and walk on a loose leash. In addition, you will learn how to perform these behaviors around other dogs, and with plenty of distractions, so that your owner can come to trust and predict your behavior under any situation.

Obedience training will also ensure one other crucial thing: your safety. An untrained dog is much more likely to run away, or dart into the street and get tangled with a Buick. Additionally, it's not your right to go anywhere or do anything you please. Some people don't want dogs in their faces while at the park with their kids, and I don't blame them. With the proper training, you will pay attention to your owner's desires, stay out of trouble, and not wander off.

Tell your owner to contact your veterinarian, who should be able to recommend a good obedience class in your area. Or, have him call the local chapter of the Humane Society, or even the local SPCA (Society for the Prevention of Cruelty to Animals). Both will offer classes

in your area. Private training facilities are also listed in the yellow pages. They're more expensive than the other suggestions, but they often have the most effective training programs. To find one, have your owner look through the yellow pages. Before enrolling you in any class, though, he or she should visit the place first, to get a feel for the classes they teach. If it feels right, give it a go.

Do me a favor; get an education, kid. Don't wait. You never know where it'll take you! After all, look how far I got!

Play-Biting Is a No-No!

Dear Gabby,

Once again, my humans have me befuddled. A ten-month-old male Akita, I live with a young couple and their two kids, a six-year-old boy and an eight-year-old girl. The kids let me nibble and play-bite on their hands and fingers while we play; I've never drawn blood, and it seems to be an effective way to let them know when I've had enough roughhousing. When the boy slaps me in the face, or pulls too hard on my tail, a quick mouthing usually puts a stop to it.

Yesterday, my male owner nearly hit the roof when he saw me grab the boy's hand and give it a little chomp. Though he must know I'd never hurt the kid, he acted as if I'd bitten his ears off! When he grabbed me by the scruff and lifted me off of the ground, I instinctively snapped at his arm, out of fright.

After that, he roared like a lion and tossed me into my crate for the rest of the day, no dinner or anything. Now the kids aren't allowed to play with me at all.

Gabby, I don't get it. No one ever minded a little play-biting before. When I was little, my owners thought it was cute, and even seemed to enjoy when I nibbled on their hands. What went wrong?

Yours, stumped,
Chopper in Chattanooga

DEAR CHOPPER,

What a mess. I think we'd all be better off if humans were made of rock, and dogs had no teeth. Trouble is, they aren't, and we do.

Here's the scoop, pork chop. Biting, even play-biting or nibbling, is a no-no. Shouldn't even be in the picture. Add little kids into the mix, and you've got a stinky dog shelter looming in your future. Besides, you are an Akita, man. Akitas are by nature dominant and territorial, and originally bred to be guard dogs. The idea of an Akita biting little kids— well, it's a turn-off, to say the least. You're a strong dude, with bone-crushing strength in those choppers of yours; no wonder the parents are freaking.

That said, most of the blame lies with (you guessed it) your adult owners, who encouraged you as a puppy to nibble and play-bite on their hands. Well, what we dogs learn early on tends to stick with us. Teach a twelve-week-old pup to chase a Frisbee all day, and he will love it for the rest of his life. Your owners mistakenly encouraged you to use your mouth and teeth on them while you were a baby, and you've continued doing that, even though you are now a nearly full-grown Akita.

The reason your male owner freaked out, Chopper, is that he thought the safety of his child was in jeopardy. A normal reaction really, though how he dealt with you was a bit ham-handed, to say the least.

First, let me say that owners should never ever encourage a puppy or adult dog to mouth, nibble, or play-bite on any part of the human anatomy. From day one, it should never be an option. A dog's teeth are for eating, and for chewing on safe chews and toys, period. When a puppy is teething, it should be provided with vet-approved chews and toys to satisfy this need. Fingers are not vet-approved chew toys, and shouldn't be on the menu.

Next, I must say that there are a few bad eggs out there, dogs who are programmed to be aggressive in some way. The vast majority of these are fear-aggressive dogs who use biting as a defense mechanism. Insecure by nature, they think they are about to be hurt, and so bite first and ask questions later. For a puppy or adult dog who shows great fear or aggression without obvious provocation, professional help from a veterinarian or canine behaviorist will be needed, and the following advice won't apply, or help.

If a normally adjusted puppy grabs a human's hand, the first thing for the human to try is to yell *"Owwwww!"* loudly. This will in no uncertain terms let most pups know that the experience was not a desirable one for you, and shouldn't be repeated. It works well with about half of the puppies out there, and is the least intrusive method of

stopping the behavior. Puppies in a litter do this with each other all the time; this is one of the ways they learn to modulate or curb the biting. Interestingly, puppies who leave their litters too soon often develop play-biting problems later on. They just never learned from their mothers or littermates to go easy.

If the yelling technique doesn't work, the owner should connect a short leash to the puppy's training collar, and give it a quick pop as soon as the pet begins to nibble or bite, while simultaneously saying *"No!"* in a commanding (though not loud) tone. This lets the puppy know that its actions are inappropriate. After this, the owner should open his or her hand, and offer it to the puppy's mouth. If the pup licks at the palm, it should be praised, and told *"Good!"* Reward the good behavior, discourage the bad.

In your case, the first thing your owners need to do is completely stop all roughhousing with you. Neither the kids nor the adults should be vying physically with you. You're an Akita, for corn sakes; they can't hope to win. Better never to challenge you physically, as it will only serve to make you more dominant and pushy. No chase games either, especially ones in which they chase after you (a very submissive thing to do). Tug-o'-war is also out.

Next, whenever the kids play with you, they *cannot* be allowed to ever pull on your tail or ears, or strike you in any way. End of story. They need to be supervised whenever near you, from now on. It's not fair to any dog to ask it to put up with such mistreatment.

If you are still foolish enough to play-bite, tell them to get a plant spray bottle, fill it with water and a tablespoon of white vinegar, and spray you right in the mouth whenever you place your mouth on someone. That should eventually break you of the habit. They shouldn't yell or hit you, as that might just make matters worse. They also should hold off on leash corrections until after taking a basic obedience class with you. A full-grown, untrained Akita might not react well to a hard leash correction from an amateur.

Finally, if the problem continues, you'll need to have them bring in a canine behaviorist to help solve the issue. These people are like doggy shrinks, Chopper; they can only help.

In the meantime, lay off the finger sandwiches, will you?

And No Jumping, Either!

Dear Gabby,

A two-year-old standard poodle, I just love my owners to death. Whenever they come home, I jump up onto their legs and paw at them, to show my undying love. It's very fulfilling, and they seem not to mind.

The problem comes when other people visit. Happy to see them too, I jump up onto their legs and beg for attention. Some of them seem amused, but others get flustered, and a few back away, throw up their arms, and act frightened. When my owners' little niece came in last week, I jumped up on her and knocked her down into the coffee table. She cut her head, and cried like a kitten. I got screamed at by everybody; now, whenever I jump up, they yell *"NO!"* and back away.

Gabby, I don't get it. I've been jumping up on people since I can remember. What went wrong?

Sincerely,

Springy in Springfield

DEAR SPRINGY,

Ah, the old leaping poodle dilemma. You French types are so full of that *joie de vivre*. Problem is, many humans don't share in your enthusiasm. Frankly, even I don't much care for a dog putting paws on me, and pushing me into next Tuesday.

Springy, when a dog gets excited and jumps up onto someone, it is usually considered to be an obnoxious invasion of privacy. It doesn't matter that the offender isn't doing it out of malice or spite; it's simply rude. That said, your owners have (as usual) done you a disservice by allowing you to jump up on them, probably from the day they got you. Cute and endearing back then, it has now become annoying, and even dangerous to some (such as kids and the elderly).

By tolerating the behavior, your owners inadvertently taught you to do it time and again, until it became the normal greeting procedure for you. Because they helped start it, they will have to help you stop it.

The following are a few techniques that you might want to pass on to your owners. If they follow my advice, the jumping behavior should be minimized, or stopped completely, within a few weeks. Tell them to read it carefully!

Method A: *Holding the dog's paws*
(Note: Do not try this with a dog who has shown any signs of aggression.)

- If a dog jumps up, calmly but firmly grasp its front paws, one in each hand, and *do not let go*. Talk to the dog calmly and do not get emotional, but make sure not to let go.
- After a few seconds, the dog will want its paws back. Do not let go yet. Just keep talking calmly. Even if it whines or mouths your hands, *keep hold.*
- After eight or ten seconds, the dog will be very annoyed and will really want you to release it. At that point, let go and simultaneously say *"Off."* When the dog's front feet touch the ground, say *"Good Off,"* and then really praise it.
- Wait a few minutes, then call the dog over again. If it jumps up on you, repeat the exercise.
- Have all members of the household practice this method, provided they are strong enough to hold onto the dog's paws. The very young may have difficulty with this.

Method B: *Using a spray bottle*
An alternative to the first method, the owner will need to purchase several plant sprayer bottles, fill them with water, and adjust them so that they emit a tight stream of water. He or she

can add a tablespoon of white vinegar to the water, if necessary. Place the bottles in areas of the home where they are easily accessible, and where the jumping most often occurs (such as the front door).

◆ Call your dog over to you (making sure to have a spray bottle in hand). If your dog jumps up, immediately spray it in the mouth and nose with the water while saying *"OFF."* When its front feet touch the floor, say *"Good Off,"* then praise it.

◆ Repeat the exercise in a few minutes. Your dog should learn very quickly not to continue jumping up on you.

◆ All members of the family as well as frequent visitors should practice this exercise. Young children should not be allowed to make a game out of spraying the dog, though, as this would be cruel and counterproductive.

Method C: *Using a leash and collar*
Some dogs will not jump up onto their own owners, but will do so with others who approach it, particularly during walks. This method works best with these types of dogs.

1. Have another person wait for you about a block down the street.

2. Clip your dog's leash onto its training collar, then go out for a walk.

3. Approach your friend. The moment your dog

begins to jump up, give the leash a quick pop toward your knees, while saying *"No, Off."* At the same time, the friend should back away a few steps. Do not become emotional; simply use a firm, commanding tone of voice.

4. Next, ask the dog to sit. As soon as it does, have your friend pet it, and give it a treat. You want the dog to eventually realize that sitting is the proper position to be in when being greeted. Whenever the dog jumps up, correct it with a firm pop on the leash. Whenever it sits to be greeted, have your friend praise it. Soon, the dog will be conditioned to perform the behavior that receives the more pleasant response, namely the pet on the head, rather than the "pop" of the leash.

5. An alternative to this method is to have two leashes clipped to the dog's collar when approaching the friend. When you are close to the friend, stop, step on the loose leash so that there is little slack in it, then have the friend come up and pet the dog. If it tries to jump up, the leash you have your foot on will instantly become taut, preventing the dog from jumping up. Be sure to maintain a grip on the other leash, to prevent the dog from running away.

Whichever technique your owners choose, Springy, it must be practiced consistently for at least six weeks, the period of time it takes to permanently modify a behavior in a dog. If they are diligent, you should stop this annoying habit pronto. It's to your advantage to do so, dog; after all, you'll learn to sit well, and you might get some treats out of it!

Freedom's Just Another Word for a Lazy Owner

Dear Gabby,

I'm a four-month-old female border collie pup, cute as a cold meat pie. Last week, I went home with a nice retired couple living in a small house in the country. Nice people, but not too hip regarding the needs of a border collie puppy. As you know, we're smart and driven, and need lots of attention and training.

Though they seem to know a bit about dogs, both let me wander about the home without much supervision. Yesterday I had to pee like an un-neutered mastiff, so I ran over to the man and did my little circle dance. Who doesn't understand the circle dance? Anyway, he just patted me on the head and went back to reading his paper! Desperate, I quietly peed in a corner of the bedroom, and then set off to find my chew toy (a nice little plastic Yoda). Unable to find it, I settled on a leather slipper, and had a mighty good chew of it.

Three hours later, Mr. Man wakes me up screaming his head off. *The carpet in the bedroom, blah blah blah, my favorite slippers, blah blah!* You know; their blessed stuff. Humans like stuff a lot, don't they?

Gabby, I'm in the dog house with these people now. What went wrong? I mean, when you gotta go, you gotta go. And chewing? Who isn't up for a good chew? Enlighten me, please.

Your bud,

Borderless in Boston

DEAR BORDERLESS,

Though you border collies tend to be a bit on the intense side, the fault here lies, as usual, with the owner, and not the dog. Any puppy (and especially a precocious little border collie) needs close supervision for several months before being given the freedom to wander the home unchecked. It doesn't sound like your owners have been doing that. The sports page, it seems, has priority over your little bladder.

Puppies and newly adopted adult dogs simply cannot be given total freedom from the get-go. They don't yet know the rules of the home, and aren't likely to be properly housetrained, either. Letting a four-month-old puppy wander about the home alone is like asking an ill-tempered Rottweiler to baby-sit the neighbor's rabbits for a few hours.

In addition to destructive behavior and housetraining mishaps, the unsupervised new dog can get itself into dangerous situations. Exposed wiring or toxic cleaners, for instance, if left out, can mean death to an unsuspecting, curious pooch, as can an open door or window.

Here's what to tell your owners, hon. First, when they can't be physically with you, you need to be in a dog crate, fenced yard, or dog kennel. When they are home, they need to keep an eye on you, and not let you wander off by yourself, a sure recipe for trouble. Tell them to clip your leash on, and then tie it to a belt loop. That way, you will always be six feet away or closer, at all times. By doing so, they will know when it's time to take you out. Also, you'll learn to pay attention to them, and bond closely.

Over a period of a few months, as your housetraining skills improve, they will be able to gradually give you more and more freedom to roam the home. Before that can happen, though, they'll need to "puppy-proof" the place. Let them know that all potentially dangerous or valuable items must be removed or hidden from your reach. These items include:

- wiring and batteries
- glass items, or anything breakable
- cleaners, solvents, detergents, paints, antifreeze, and all other toxins
- edible plants
- leather items
- money
- jewelry
- remote control devices
- clothing (especially dirty socks and underwear)
- human foods (particularly chocolate, a known toxin to cats and dogs)
- garbage (ideally placed behind a cupboard with childproof locks)
- all human medicines
- human toys

Tell them to close windows and doors, and to not trust screens, easily pushed out by most dogs. Also, every dog should be provided with veterinarian-approved chews and chew toys, to help relieve stress and satisfy the desire to chew, especially strong among teething puppies. If they aren't doing so, let them know! You're a border collie; you'll find a way.

A lazy, overly trusting owner asks for trouble by giving his or her puppy the run of the house from day one. By supervising closely and gradually allowing more and more freedom over time, owners stand a much better chance of developing in us dogs acceptable house manners. And, one more thing, hon; see what you can do about getting a few wayward sheep into your life.

The All-Important Unmentionable (Neutering)

Dear Gabby,

I'm writing you from dog jail, where I've been now for three days straight, pending some sort of ruling. Not a good week, let me tell you.

A one-year-old male bull mastiff, I live up in the Hollywood Hills, in a great house. My owners are in show biz; loaded to the gills, baby, with a pool and servants and a big wrought-iron gate, and all sorts of people coming and going, night and day. That's part of the problem, Gabby; as a bull mastiff, I'm supposed to protect the home, right? It's what we do best as a breed, and one of the reasons that they got me in the first place.

For the last three or four months, I've grown quite a bit, and have stopped acting like a puppy toward everyone. I particularly hate when the gardeners come on Mondays. They storm through the gate in the morning and start roaming all over the place, as if they owned it. Recently, I have been letting them know just how I feel, mostly by barking and

growling from inside the house, where the maid
keeps me on Monday mornings.

Last Monday (three days ago), while sweep-
ing the patio, the maid left the back door open
long enough for me to get out. Though she tried
to catch me, she's the size of a dog biscuit,
and not too fast. Anyway, I stomped over to the
gardener's truck, peed on it (hadn't since the
night before, so . . .), then gave those gate-
crashers a piece of my mind.

One of them ran away screaming, so I of
course chased him. He turned and started winging
a shovel at me, so I ducked, then bit him on
the butt a few times. Then I went after the
other guys, who by this time had locked themselves in their truck. The guy I bit jumped into
the pool and stayed there until the cops came. I
don't even want to *talk* about that scene.

Now the uniformed guys here whisper as
they walk by my kennel. I can't quite make it
out, but one keeps saying "neuter" over and
over, as he shakes his head.

Gabby, did I do something wrong? And what
does "neuter" mean?

Your perplexed pooch,
Prisoner in Paradise

DEAR JAILBIRD,

Ugh. What a mess. Look, this macho thing isn't all it's cut out to be, pal, believe me. When I was young, I once chased the new mail carrier down the street. Felt great. Next thing I knew, I was in the waiting room at the veterinarian's office. And no, it wasn't to have my temperature taken.

The celebs you call owners know bupkis about dogs, and certainly didn't put much effort into choosing a breed. Anyone intending to have lots of guests and strangers milling about his or her home should get either a golden retriever, or a Siamese cat.

You're right about bull mastiffs; you guys were bred to guard, and to protect. Now, that doesn't mean you can't learn to accept guests; with the proper training and socialization, you could become a great ambassador. But it takes work, and one other ingredient which you aren't going to like hearing, something your owners should have taken care of three or four months ago.

One of the most effective ways to minimize aggression or dominance in any dog, male or female, is to have the pet neutered before its seventh or eighth month. Now, cross your legs and grab hold of the fence, Prisoner, because this won't be easy for you. Neutering (castration of a male, or spaying of a female) involves the surgical removal of the dog's reproductive organs (males have their testes removed, while females lose their ovaries and uterus). Doing so puts an abrupt end to the production of male or female hormones, which, particularly in males, stimulate dominant, aggressive, or territorial behaviors. You know, that macho thang.

In addition to reducing aggressive behaviors, neutering has other major benefits, including:

◆ Easier training
◆ Fewer housetraining or marking mishaps
◆ Less chance of roaming or escaping
◆ No unwanted puppies
◆ Fewer incidences of cancer and other serious diseases
◆ Longer life span

Sorry to say, pal, but unless you are a champion show dog who is in high demand on the stud circuit (you wish), your owners should have you neutered as soon as possible. Doing so will reduce your drive to kill gardener types, and will make training and managing you much easier. You'll live longer, and have less stress in your life. I had it done a long time ago, and, between you and me, I really don't miss them, dude.

After the trip to the vet, your owners will have to get real, and attend an obedience class with you. Hopefully, in addition to learning how to control you, they will begin to understand that socialization is also a key ingredient in minimizing protective, suspicious canine behaviors. You need to learn that most people and other dogs are not out to get you, man.

Peace, bro, and good luck at the vet.

To Protect or Not to Protect: That Is the Question

Dear Gabby,

I've had a tough life, and I think it just got tougher. A six-month-old female pit bull mix, I was bred by a drug dealer in Brooklyn, and sold to an addict at the age of four weeks. When he was busted last month, I went to a "no-kill" shelter in the suburbs, where they took care of me and worked on my fear-aggression problem.

Gabby, confrontation scares the hell out of me. The only time I ever get violent is when I feel threatened, which seems to be almost all the time these days. Problem is, I was just recently adopted by a family that wants me to protect their home, located near a high-crime area. They're nice, but I just don't feel up to the job.

During the day I am kept chained in the front yard, while they are at work and school. All day, strange people walk by. Some try to pet me through the fence, while others taunt and tease me. I growl and snap at all of them, and wish I could just run away.

At night they bring me inside. It's better in there, but when they go to bed, they leave me out in the living room to watch over the place. I spend the night beneath the sofa, growling at the street traffic.

Gabby, I'm not the dog they think I am. They want a guard dog, but then take me to the park on weekends, to play and socialize with their friends. I'm scared; what should I do?

Yours sincerely,

Anxious in Astoria

DEAR ANXIOUS,

Ugh. Tough one here. I swear, some humans really do deserve a good bite on the ass. Sorry for all your troubles, hon. Let me try to address them.

Drug dealers and addicts often get attack dogs to protect themselves, their goods, and their pads. Others get dogs with macho reputations (pit bulls, Rottweilers, Dobermans, German shepherds) in order to appear tougher than they are. Still others breed or buy tough dogs in order to fight them, a disgusting spectacle that always leads to misery and death for the animals. These are bad people who should never, ever own a dog.

Even caring people can contribute to the problem, however. Many obtain dogs for protection against burglars and other bad people trying to hurt or rob them. Not a bad idea, really, at first thought. The problem comes when they get the dog home. Some dogs might not have the disposition to protect, while others can't distinguish between good people and bad, and simply attack everyone. Still others are improperly treated and trained by owners, who want to make the dog tougher, or more attentive to danger.

Problem is, the average human knows nothing about how to train a dog to protect or guard, while still remaining calm and controlled during times of safety. Professional dog trainers know how to program a well-bred dog for this, but getting the right dog and the right training can cost many thousands of dollars.

Most people don't go that route; instead, they go to the pound and adopt a pit bull or Rottweiler, and hope for the best. Often, all they end up with is a scared, dangerous animal incapable of telling safe persons from dangerous ones.

I don't think it's fair for owners to expect a dog to protect a home. We'll surely bark if someone tries to break in, but why should we be expected to dodge bullets and play the hero all day and night?

Generally, any dog capable of taking down two or three armed intruders isn't going to be the kind of pet who will easily interact with a family, or their friends. Ninety-nine percent of the time, life with a dog like that will be hell. A poorly adjusted, aggressive dog left loose in a yard will almost certainly attack a child foolish enough to climb the fence and drop in to get a lost ball. Most aggressive dogs aren't even confident, predictable pets; rather, they are more often fearful animals who attack at the slightest provocation, even if no real threat is present. What owner would want that time bomb in the home?

Your situation is a sad one, Anxious. You had bad beginnings, and never got properly socialized with people or dogs. You have classic fear aggression, which can only be dealt with by an experienced canine behaviorist, and lots of care

and love on the part of your owners. Fear-aggressive dogs won't properly protect a home; rather, they'll usually just hide under the bed and whine.

Convince your owners to take you to a qualified canine behaviorist, to deal with your psychological baggage. They also have to get you out of the yard, and off of that chain, as both only serve to magnify your dread. Right now, you shouldn't be taken into big crowds of people and dogs, as that's just going to freak you out, and perhaps cause a biting incident.

If they want to protect their home, let them get an alarm, or sign up with a security service. They can take karate, buy a bazooka, or move to a better neighborhood. My advice to humans: Get a dog for companionship, not warfare.

Tales of Trouble

TRAINING MISTAKES

I'm the first to admit that we dogs need guidance and structure in our lives, if we are going to make it in this crazy human world. A gazillion years ago, we could have just gone out and done our canine thing, hunting down animals and running around like action heroes all of the time. Simple instinct would have been the guiding force. But today, we live in a complicated and sometimes dangerous world, one run by wacky humans with cars and fences and all sorts of crazy laws. They are the pack leaders now, poochies, and we need to abide by their rules, however bizarre, if we are going to survive.

Problem is, most owners don't do a very good job of teaching us what to do, and when to do it. Most of them don't even know what it is they *do* want us to do. In general, they tend to be inconsistent, and a bit ignorant of canine needs and instincts. They either baby the heck out of us, or else treat us like doo-doo.

Their inability to train us correctly (or at all) results in all types of problems for us, and for them. Lost dogs, flaring tempers, antisocial episodes, and outright disobedience can occur when an owner shirks his or her training responsibilities. And in the end, who gets blamed? You guessed it, hairball.

Part Two contains letters that touch upon some key issues of training, which, when mishandled by owners, can cause trouble for everyone, especially you. If my suggestions are heeded, though, "La Dolce Vita" can be right around the corner. Read them carefully, then leave the book out for the two-foots to find.

Hitting Is Never Right!

Dear Gabby,

I'm a two-year-old giant schnauzer male with a migraine. Yesterday, about an hour or so before dinner, I happened to wander into the kitchen to find a steaming meatloaf up on the counter. Gabby, it smelled so good, I just had to steal a look. Standing on my hind legs, I soon found myself eye to eye with the tender, fragrant beast.

Next thing I know, I get whomped in the head so hard I see stars. Falling to the floor, I see my owner standing there, broom in hand, yelling and screaming. Needless to say, I hightailed it out of there, and hid under the sofa for the rest of the night.

Gabby, is the meatloaf a sacred icon to the humans? Did I do something profane? Tell me what to do!

Yours cautiously,

KO'd in Camden

DEAR KO'D,

Down for the count, eh? Sorry, big fella. In answer to your question, yes, humans throughout the ages have held the mysterious meatloaf in high esteem. Best not to ever covet one again.

Problem is, the whole ugly incident could have been easily avoided if your careless owner had taken a modicum of precautions. When leaving food out on tables or counters, an owner should always make sure that all pets are safely out of the area. If a particularly tempting item is present, it should not be left unattended at any time. What do they expect us to do, for heaven's sake? Are we not dogs?

Now to the more serious issue. After setting you up to fail, your owner committed the ultimate sin by swatting you in the head with that broom. Shame! Using physical violence to punish a dog should never be an option, unless the safety of another human is in serious jeopardy. All it teaches a dog is to fear its owner, and to potentially show fear aggression in the future. You could have been severely hurt, or even killed, had the weapon been a bit heavier.

The best way to deal with the situation would have been to give you a severe verbal reprimand, then put you in your crate or kennel for a while. For a dog with a track record of bad behavior, a leash should be clipped onto its training collar while in the home; any improper behavior could then be punished with a sharp leash correction and a

"No!" Afterwards, the bad dog could be made to perform a "Stay" for ten or twenty minutes, somewhere within sight of the owner.

Bad behavior needs to be reprimanded in the proper way. Verbal warnings, leash corrections, a squirt from a hose or spray bottle, or even a loud clap are all efficient methods to let a dog know it's made a boo-boo. Hitting only serves to scare and hurt, and proves that some humans are at best poor leaders, and at worst sadistic.

Beware of those meatloaf-coveting humans, KO'd, and stay out of the kitchen.

Why We Need to
Act Obediently

Dear Gabby,

Everything seemed great at first. Nice family, big yard, three squares, huge house. They
came to the breeder's and picked me up on a
nice, sunny day, the kids all happy and excited. It seemed, well--perfect.

And it was, for a while. As a puppy, I was
small, and manageable. But female Chesapeake
Bay retrievers get big, fast, and I was no ex-
ception. I grew in size and strength, until,
at six months of age, I was bigger than the
twelve-year-old girl.

The breeder had told them to get me
obedience trained, but I guess they didn't
listen. Soon, I was tearing about the place,
breaking things, jumping up on guests, and escaping whenever I could. Without any training
or direction, a high-energy dog like me was
bound to get on somebody's nerves. When I
shredded the seats in the Beemer, they went
ballistic.

Now I'm back at the breeder's, living in a
crate in the garage. There's no one to play

with except for Mom, who doesn't seem to remember me very well. Gabby, what went wrong? I
had such promise, such potential. Now all I do
is dream of duck ponds and German sedans. Help!

Humbly,

Homeless in Houston

DEAR HOMELESS,

All revved up and no ducks to fetch, huh? Sorry, lady. You're just another unfortunate victim of the inability of humans to understand what dogs need to get by in the world.

Like other sporting breeds, "Chessies" are bred to have lots of energy. This vigor needs to be controlled and channeled properly, in order to help the dog exist in the human world. Obedience training is an absolutely essential ingredient in accomplishing this.

We dogs look for order and leadership in our lives. We want to look up to someone, for guidance and direction. Democracy? Not in the canine world. We respond better to the benevolent dictator than to the city council. Hail Caesar!

When Caesar can't be found, we become stressed, and a little crazy. Often, with no apparent leader in sight, we attempt to take on the role ourselves. This causes chaos for the humans in the home, who can't understand why we aren't obeying. No matter how they plead, we just keep eating up the upholstery.

Though they meant well, your owners never followed through on the breeder's sage advice to get you trained. If they had done so, they could have controlled you, and given you a sense of security to boot. With a confident leader showing you how to behave, life would have been easier for everyone. Instead, they neglected to teach you anything, and left you to your own devices. What's a retriever to do?

From day one, owners need to start working with their puppies, teaching them to sit, lie down, stay, and come on command. Doing so allows them to control us, and at the same time gives us the confidence and leadership a pack animal craves. Without it, disaster looms.

Don't worry, Homeless; I am sure your breeder will teach you the basics before letting anyone take you home again. He or she won't want you to end up at the dog pound, waiting for that grim reaper to come calling. Good luck, water girl!

Learn to Love Your Leash

Dear Gabby,

A six-year-old male shepherd mix, I've just about had it with my new owner, who adopted me last week. He's a loud, heavy-handed dude, and our relationship has been downhill the whole way.

Where do I begin? First, when he wants my attention, he calls out some weird name that I've never heard before. When I don't respond, the ruffian yells at the top of his lungs, then chases me down, grabs my collar, and drags me over to wherever he wanted me to be. Rude, and uncalled for.

Yesterday, I made the big mistake of jumping up onto his bed. You would've thought the Visigoths had invaded. He grabbed me by the collar, dragged me off of the bed and out of the room, then screamed his bloody head off. Gave me a headache.

This morning was the topper. Seeing the cupboard door to the kitchen trash open, I innocently sniffed at it (what's a dog to do?), and again incurred his wrath. Screaming, he threw in a smack on the butt for good measure.

Well, I've been hit before, and I don't like
it one bit, so I snarled at him, bared my
teeth, then hid under the sofa for the rest of
the afternoon.

Gabby, what should I do? I don't want to
end up in the shelter again, but this guy
knows ditty about dogs. Help!

Unhappily yours,

Harried in Hoboken

DEAR HARRIED,

My kingdom for a leash! Honestly, this guy could go to the pet shop, spend twelve bucks on a leash and collar, and end the drama.

Sounds like this dude has a communications problem. When one of us goes to a new home, we don't know the house rules yet, and must be taught, quickly and fairly, in order for everyone to get along. The owner must understand that he or she needs to praise good behavior, while dissuading the bad as efficiently as possible, without anger, pain, or undue emotion. Ideally, much of this should be done with a leash.

All new dogs, be they pups or seniors, should wear a collar (with a proper ID tag), and have a short leash clipped to it *while inside the home*. That's right, inside. Why? Simple: having a three or four-foot leash always clipped on makes the owner's job of teaching and directing easy. If you jump up onto the bed, your knucklehead owner, instead of losing his cool, can simply say *"No, Off,"* then grab the leash and guide you off the bed. If you go up there again, he can add a quick little pop on the leash, and a bit sterner reproach. Soon, you will understand that the bed is verboten. No temper, no pleading, no violence; just unemotional control.

The same could have been done with the trash calamity. Upon seeing you nosing around the garbage, he could have simply said *"No, Leave It,"* given the leash a tiny pop, then guided you away to an appropriate spot. No grabbing you by the collar or scruff (a very threatening move), or hitting you. Instead, an unemotional, corrective maneuver on his part.

The same leash protocol should be used when outdoors. If a dog is misbehaving or becoming a nuisance in public, the owner can simply give the pooch a small leash correction, say *"No,"* then guide the dog away, without grabbing or hitting. This teaches the dog what is appropriate behavior.

When an owner yells or manhandles, he or she teaches nothing except the expectation of fear and pain. This can lead to distrust, additional misbehaviors, fear aggression, or a runaway dog. Why go through that? Plus, while one of us dogs is running around misbehaving, our owner can't catch us, and so cannot stop the behavior, which becomes self-reinforcing. The dog continues the bad behavior unabated, teaching itself to continue performing the bad act.

By keeping a leash on a new dog 24/7 (for at least two or three months), an owner can teach and guide the pooch through that difficult period with a minimum of emotion and conflict. While indoors, the leash can be as short as two feet in length. Outdoors, a four to six foot leash works best. Tell your owner to read the next letter for info on using longer leads for recall work.

Hang in there, Harried, and leave this reply on the coffee table for your emotional owner to find. Who knows? It just might give you both a new leash on life.

Learning Your Recall Command

Dear Gabby,

I'm a perky, seven-month-old female whippet. We love to run, and yesterday I got my chance to prove it. My owner let me off the leash for the first time at a sprawling, busy park. Ten seconds later I was half a mile away chasing geese into the lake, and toying with an amorous old lab who likes his women thin. Good thing I'm fast, as I haven't been spayed yet.

I had a great day, but I guess my owner didn't. She found me around sunset, playing with some kids in a parking lot. You'd have thought somebody gave up the ghost, by the look on her face. Instead of being happy to see me, she grabbed me by the ear, clipped my leash on, and dragged me off to the car.

I hadn't been out of the house in days, Gabby, except to go #1 and #2 in the fenced yard. Yesterday at the park was so much fun; what's going on?

Yours truly,

Revved Up in Reno

DEAR REVVED,

Sure is fun to run free, ain't it? Problem is, humans can't move as fast as us dogs. Plus, being on the young side, you don't yet understand just how dangerous the human world can be. Luckily, you were in a big park, away from the cars and crazies.

Though you shouldn't have left your owner high and dry like that, you really didn't know any better. The real blame for this great escape lies with your owner, who should have known not to let a young, untrained dog off the leash in a public place.

Now, I'm sure you know the basics like "Sit" and "Down," but obviously you don't yet comprehend the command "Come," at least not when given in such a fun, stimulating environment as a busy park. Until you do, your owner shouldn't ever let a headstrong speedster like yourself off the leash.

The "Come" is perhaps the hardest and most important command your owner will ever teach you. Obeying it without hesitation may literally save your skinny little butt one day. Until you do, you absolutely MUST be on a leash when outside the safety of your home or yard.

Here is how your owner should go about training you to come on command. Show this to her as soon as possible:

◆ In the beginning, you and your owner should work the "Come" inside the home, with you on a six-foot leash.

A quiet area should be used, with no other persons present to break your concentration. First, she should place
you in a sitting position, slowly back away from you,
then crouch down and happily say *"Come!"* The moment you do, she should give you a cookie, and say
"Good Come!" If you decide to blow her off for some
reason, she can pop the leash slightly, say *"No,"* then repeat the command. If you still ignore her, she can literally force you to come to her, by reeling you in. The
leash is vital at this stage, as it ensures that you will
come to her *every time,* no matter what. By learning
that you have no other choice, you will quickly accept
the inevitability of the situation.

◆ Once you are coming to her every time inside the
home, your owner should work the exercise in the yard,
still using the leash. As distractions abound outdoors,
you may tend to ignore her a few times, until you again
realize that you have no other choice.

◆ Once you are performing the short "Come" in the yard,
it's time to lengthen the leash. Have her get a twenty-
foot piece of rope, or purchase one of those retractable
leashes at the pet store. She should attach either to your
collar, then, still in the yard, wander away from you,
until you become distracted by something. Then, from
the end of the long lead, she should crouch down and
call you over to her in a happy voice. If you do not

immediately respond, you get corrected. Then, she should repeat the command. When you finally do come, she should praise you and reward you with a treat. If you refuse to come to her, she has the option of literally reeling you in. Again, no choice but to obey. Have her also let a friend or family member hang out in the yard while this is going on, for added distraction.

◆ Once this stage is perfected, it's time for her to clip the leash off, and try an off-leash "Come," in the yard. Only until this is perfected with distraction should a speedster like you ever be allowed off-leash in public. If you do not "Come" reliably, every time, she should go back to using the long lead.

◆ Finally, she should take you to a large fenced-in area (tennis courts work great), and work your off-leash "Come." Again, if you backslide, the long lead goes back on, to ensure obedience every time. Make sure she understands that, if you ever get the chance to ignore this command without retribution, you will quickly learn to disobey.

Once this final stage is perfected, you should be ready to again chase those poopy geese. Just don't tease the randy old lab, though; he's only doing what the big Alpha in the sky intended him to do.

Abusing the Recall Command: Praise or Punishment?

Dear Gabby,

I'm not sure I know right from wrong anymore. A three-year-old female retriever mix, I learned my recall command very quickly, as most retrievers do. In the past, whenever I'd hear my owner yell out the *"Come"* command, I'd be on him like ticks on a bloodhound, every time. But lately, he's been calling me over and then punishing me for this or that. For instance, when I got into the garbage yesterday, he found the mess, called me over, then read me the riot act. And last week, he called me into the bedroom and then yelled at me for jumping up onto the bed earlier in the day (I haven't quite mastered making the bed yet).

Gabby, I can't even enjoy a good fetch anymore. I know I'm supposed to come to my owner when called, but why should I, if he's only going to punish me when I do? When I hear that word *"Come"* now, I hide under the sofa and shiver. Have I dropped the ball on this one?

Truly,

Irretrievable in Indianapolis

DEAR IRRETRIEVABLE,

I wish I could get a leash and collar onto one of them, just once. Seriously, sometimes they are clueless regarding cause and effect. Your owner has committed a big training mistake, and might live to regret it big time some day soon, unless he changes his ways pronto. Let me explain.

The recall, or *"Come"* command, is arguably the most important behavior an owner can teach to a dog. Why? Because it can save a pooch's life. Think about it; you're running around in front of your home, and a truck is barreling down the street at sixty. In your retriever excitement, you head for the street to chase after a tennis ball. Know what? That truck ain't going to stop for you, pal. If you two intersect, it's going to be road stew.

The only way to prevent that from happening is for you to instantly respond to your owner's command to come to him. There can't be any hesitation; it must be immediate, and unfaltering. If you hesitate for even a second, you'll be greasing the tires of that Peterbilt.

Tell you a quick story. When I was a tyke, my first owner taught me the recall, and I performed it flawlessly, every time. One day, while hiking together in the Santa Monica mountains, I took the lead, and was having a grand old time sniffing and exploring. Then, just ahead of me, I saw a big stick in the trail. Then, to my amazement, the stick began to move! Being a pup, I just had to check it out. As I got close enough to get a good sniff, I heard my owner call to me. Her voice had an urgency in it I'd not heard before, so I turned tail and returned to her. As I happily greeted her, I noticed she was crying. She petted and kissed me, then clipped on my leash, and as we walked around the stick, I saw that it wasn't a stick at all, but a big old rattlesnake! One good sniff and I would have been chasing cats in paradise. The point of my story is this: If I hadn't been trained and encouraged to come on command, I would have been killed that day.

Instead of teaching you to come confidently, your owner has undermined the behavior by punishing you after obediently coming to him. He thinks he is simply reprimanding you for an inappropriate behavior (stay out of the garbage and off the bed, dude!), but in reality he is teaching you *not to come*. Why would any dog continue to come on command if, after doing so, its owner blew his top?

Instead of calling you to him and then punishing you, he should have simply found you, clipped your leash on, led you over to the transgression, then reprimanded you. That way, the *"Come"* command is not utilized at all, and therefore not undermined. That way, when he really needs you to come to him, you'll do so without fear of reprisal. So, in answer to your question, Irretrievable, it's not your fault, though you should lay off the trash, and learn to make the bed.

On Being a Socialite

Dear Gabby,

I'm a six-year-old male Chihuahua who's sick of strangers coming over to the house in the evening. Who do they think they are, invading my territory? I especially hate when they try to pet me. I don't know them or like them; why should they be able to touch me?

Except for the yard, my owner rarely takes me out, and frankly that's fine with me. I'd rather just stay home. It's just too upsetting for me out there. I like our home, and would prefer it if no one ever came over.

During the day, I stay at home, by myself. Sometimes I look out the window and bark at nosy people passing by. The barking seems to work, as they keep walking, and leave the house alone.

Lately though, my owner has been getting on my case for growling and nipping at guests. He seems to want me to like *everybody*. Hey, do I look like a golden retriever? Well, I'll tell you this much; I am *not* going in the water, and I will not wear one of those lame bandanas around my neck.

Gabby, is it me, or am I justified in being grumpy? Do I have to let people rub their grimy hands all over me? And what's with the kissy-kissy stuff? I do *not* want to kiss them. Who knows where their mouths have been?

Yours always,

Aloof in Altoona

DEAR ALOOF,

I had a Chihuahua buddy back when I was riding the rails. He lived in a shack near the freight yard, outside of Chattanooga. Crabby old cuss. Didn't like anybody except me, his hobo, and a stray poodle babe he had the hots for. He lived to be about twenty, I think. One day I found him stiff as a board, inside of a rusty bucket filled with stinky rags. Guess he used to sleep in there. Saddest thing I ever saw.

What I'm trying to say is, why live life all alone, save for one or two family members? After all, are we not dogs?

You being so antisocial is really not your fault, pal. For years, your owner left you home alone, day and night, ignoring a dog's need to socialize. Eventually, you grew to distrust anyone who even came close to the home, seeing them as trespassers into your domain. With no socialization, you became withdrawn, protective, and suspicious. Hey, that's what happens when you don't get out.

Your owner goofed. He figured that, because you were a small dog, you wouldn't need to get out much. You didn't go for walks, and never got to the park to play with other dogs and meet other people. You began to view the occasional visitor as a threat and a bother, instead of a welcome social event. Eventually, the home and your owner became the only things in your life worth wagging your tail over.

No dog should be starved for regular social experiences.

We are pack animals by nature, and need to get out there and interact, from an early age. Without doing so, we become withdrawn, and wary. Your growling and nipping at guests is a natural reaction of a dog long denied any meaningful socialization.

Your owner should have gotten you out of the house, pal. Each and every dog, from puppyhood on, should:

◆ Go for a walk or two each day.

◆ Get to a dog park once every week, to play and socialize with other friendly dogs

◆ Interact with people in as many different venues as possible, and

◆ Learn to accept the presence of other humans in the home, by having friendly guests come over regularly.

You know what? It's not too late for you. You little guys live forever; there's still time to mend your ways. Your owner needs to:

◆ Take you for at least one walk each day, around the neighborhood, for at least fifteen minutes. You don't have to let people pet you; just seeing them from a distance is enough right now.

◆ Take you to an area where other dogs

congregate. You needn't interact if you choose not to; all you need to do is see them playing happily.

◆ Allow other humans to walk you on a regular basis. They don't have to pet you; simply walking you is enough for now.

◆ Have guests to the home avoid contact with you, other than to drop a treat at your feet. If this is done regularly, of course you will begin to look forward to strangers coming over.

◆ Regularly reward you with treats whenever you are in a social situation.

◆ Have someone come over to the home during the day, to give you a few treats, and perhaps let you out to relieve yourself. He or she needn't pet you; just being around on a regular basis will help defuse your fears.

By slowly desensitizing you to the presence of others, your owner should be able to alter your antisocial ways. You won't be throwing any garden parties soon, but at least you'll be better able to tolerate the presence of strangers. Good luck, big guy.

Consistency Rules!

Dear Gabby,

I think my owner has gone over the falls. One day she lets me jump up onto the bed or sofa, and the next she's screaming at me to get off. Sometimes she lets me have bits of food from her dinner plate, while at other times she shoos me away. It's enough to drive this old cocker spaniel bonkers.

Gabby, I can't tell what's right and what's wrong anymore. Am I going senile, or is she?

Your concerned fan,

Clueless in Cleveland

DEAR CLUELESS,

In case you haven't noticed, humans aren't the most consistent blokes in the animal kingdom. Unlike dogs, who prefer dinner, walks, and lights out at about the same time each day, people tend to be impulsive, and unpredictable. I guess that's partly why we love them. One day they adore you, and the next they can't stand the smell of your breath. It makes no sense, but it's the way it is.

It sounds as if your owner is inconsistent with rules regarding your behavior. She hasn't really figured out what is appropriate or inappropriate for you, and seems to be operating in a capricious, ill-conceived manner. Whatever appeals to her at the moment is what is okay, it seems.

This drives us dogs nuts. We like consistency in our lives, because it makes us feel happy and at ease. We look forward to things. In our book, predictability equals contentment. How would she feel if you licked her hand one day, then bit it the next? A bit unsure, I would guess.

In order for a dog to behave well, it has to be taught a clear set of fixed rules. If it's no begging at the table, it's *no begging,* period. If she hates it when you jump up onto the bed, then she should never let you do it. How else can you know what to expect? Why should you comfortably sit beside her on the sofa when, just yesterday, she screamed bloody murder when you jumped up there to cuddle with her? Hello?

Your owner clearly does not understand that dog law needs to be established and enforced consistently, in order for you to make sense of her wacky, complex world. She needs to decide what is allowable and what is not, and then stick to those decisions.

I've written some guidelines for her, Clueless. Show them to her; if she follows them, life should get a bit easier for both of you:

- ◆ Set the rules of the house, and then stick by them. If it's no begging at the table, then it's never any begging at the table! If you want your dog to walk without pulling on the leash, then he can never do so without being reprimanded. See?
- ◆ Try to set distinct times for your dog's important activities. Dinner, walks, potty breaks, and bedtime should all happen at about the same time each day.
- ◆ Try not to vary your dog's menu too quickly, as doing so can cause diarrhea. If necessary, change the type of food served gradually, over a two-week period.
- ◆ Once your dog understands what a word means, do not change the meaning of the word, or use a different word for the same command. If *"Sit"* means lower your butt down to the ground, don't suddenly say *"Hammer"* to get the dog to sit, and expect him to understand.

◆ If correcting your dog for a misbehavior, do not vary the intensity of the correction for the same level of infraction. If your pet refuses to sit on Tuesday, for instance, and gets a light leash correction because of it, don't correct him five times as hard on Wednesday for not sitting.

◆ Use a consistent, calm demeanor when working your dog. Don't be composed on one day, and a holy terror on the next. That isn't fair, and drives dogs nuts. Stay cool and predictable. It's not fair to lay your baggage on your dog!

Don't worry, Clueless; once she reads the above list, things should improve. Though they're not very predictable creatures, they do love us, and want to keep us happy. And, best of all, they have jobs.

Don't Forget to Learn Your Tricks!

Dear Gabby,

I am so bored. There is absolutely nothing to do around here. A two-year-old Australian shepherd female, I'm not exactly a dim bulb, but lately I feel, well, incompetent. The poodle across the street gets to play, fetch, do "sit-stays" in the front yard, and all sorts of other cool stuff. Me? I lick my bowl 223 times, walk around, sleep, drink water, nose print all the windows, and bark at the mail carrier.

It doesn't exactly liven up when my owners get home, either. I get to go out and eat, but that's about it. They always seem too tired, and end up paying more attention to the television than to me.

Gabby, I could be herding sheep in the outback, but instead I'm yawning and wondering how the sofa would look on the opposing wall. Tell me is that all there is, my friend?

Sincerely (bored),

Humdrum in Harrisburg

DEAR HUMDRUM,

Feeling like a Ferrari in the garage, eh? I know the feeling. During my carny days, I used to perform three shows a day for the adoring crowds. Balancing atop a beach ball, flips, unicycle—I did it all. When the carnival shut down, I was given to an old couple whose idea of fun was to watch pie cool. I was so bored, I ran away and rode the rails for a year.

Most dogs aren't given any real "jobs" to do anymore, and are instead asked to lie around the house much of the day, without purpose or direction. When no intellectual outlet is given, problems can occur. A bored, inactive pooch can become:

- stressed, depressed, and physically ill
- destructive
- disobedient and disrespectful
- old before its time

As an intelligent creature, you need an outlet for your creative and physical sides. Think of wolves in the wild; they run, jump, plan hunting strategies, play games, mate, raise young, explore, and socialize. They have complex, stimulating lives.

Unfortunately, most domestic dogs don't. They lie around and become dullards, or get stressed out from lack of mental and physical activity, which often leads to behavioral problems. What's the answer?

How about getting your owners to teach you some tricks? Doing so will:

- ◆ stimulate your mind, and give you something to look forward to
- ◆ create a stronger emotional bond between you and your owners
- ◆ teach you how to *think*, instead of simply *react to situations*
- ◆ relieve boredom and reduce stress
- ◆ create focus

Learning tricks will teach you to pay better attention, something most owners find extremely hard to teach to their pets. Like a young child waiting for you to take him or her to the ball field, you will learn to look forward to those certain times of the day when the two of you work together on a few fun tricks.

A buddy of mine down the street is a Seeing Eye dog. This guy knows *eighty-six* words, and all the accompanying behaviors. Smart as a whip, and worldly, too. If he can learn that many new words and behaviors, you can learn a few tricks.

So, what tricks should they teach you? There are a million of them. Some old standards include:

- ◆ Shake
- ◆ Wave
- ◆ Roll over
- ◆ Bark on command
- ◆ Fetch
- ◆ Spin

TALES OF TROUBLE 97

It's really up to them which ones they teach you. They can go out and buy a how-to book on dog tricks, or just wing it. The great thing about learning tricks is that they aren't necessary behaviors (like *"Stay"* or *"Come"*); if you don't get them right away, who cares? No corrections or negative reinforcement needed. You just learn at your own pace.

The following trick is one that every dog can learn. I've written down the method for them; if they follow the steps carefully, you should be performing it in no time. The only rule for them to remember is, *never use punishment of any kind when teaching a trick to your pooch.* It's all for fun. Any heavy-handedness will turn fun time into run time, so tell them to keep it light!

The "Shake" trick:

1. Put your dog into a sitting position atop a section of carpeting. A slippery surface will distract the dog and make working the trick difficult.
2. While holding a treat in your left hand, reach out with your *right hand* and lift your dog's *right* foot, while saying *"Shake."* Once you have lifted the dog's foot in your hand, say *"Good Shake,"* then reward with a small treat. Continue practicing this technique several times each day for two days before moving on.

3. Next, graduate to lightly tapping on the back of your dog's right foot several times with a finger or two, while saying *"Shake."* The goal here is to coax your dog into lifting that foot on its own. Make sure that you deliver the instigating tap directly to the back side of the dog's "wrist." If you cannot coax the dog to lift up its foot at all, then simply continue to pick its paw up in your hand, again saying *"Shake"* as you do this. *Any* movement of the dog's paw at this point, whether on its own or caused by you, should be rewarded with a small treat and happy-sounding praise. Say *"Good shake,"* even if you had to pick the paw up.

4. As you continue to work the previous step, gradually *reduce* the amount of tapping pressure applied to the back of the dog's wrist. If you had to initiate the trick by actually picking the dog's paw up in your hand, you should now try to graduate from that to the simple tap on the back of the wrist. The whole idea is to use less and less instigating pressure, eventually getting the dog to lift its paw simply upon the anticipation of you offering your hand, with no actual contact on your part. Remember to reward *any* attempt by the dog to lift its paw, even if it is just an inch or two. You want to get that "light" to go off in the dog's head;

let the pooch figure out that whenever it lifts the paw up, it gets a reward and lots of praise. *Action, consequence.* That's what conditioned response is all about. The offering of your hand will eventually become the hand signal for the trick.

5. Once the dog begins to lift its paw on its own when you offer your hand and say *"shake,"* begin offering your hand from a slightly farther distance. The objective is to now get the dog to respond to the command without your having to coax it with actual touching. Try using less hand action while giving the "shake" command, and reward any positive response. Eventually you should get the dog to offer its paw simply by your giving the verbal command and holding your hand out from a normal distance.

6. After the dog learns to shake in this way, you can next teach it to respond only to the hand signal, with no vocal command at all. Simply offer your hand, and reward any lifting response.

7. Once you have the dog performing the shake with confidence, begin to reduce the frequency of the treat reward, replacing it with verbal or physical praise. Using treats intermittently at this stage will now actually strengthen the dog's performance, because it encourages a heightened expectation.

Humdrum, if your owners work on this for a week or so, they should soon have you shaking hands with everyone in the neighborhood! Eventually they can teach you other tricks, too. Believe me, for a dog like you, the sky's the limit. When they come home, you can flaunt your stuff, and show them what an Aussie can really do. Until then, *G'day, mate!*

Surviving Children

Dear Gabby,

Any chance the schools might be going to year-round classes soon? Because if they don't, I might just have to hit the road.

Just adopted by a big family, I'm a grateful male chow chow mix up to my ears in four young kids. Ear-pulling, tail-grabbing, eye-poking kids. They're not evil, per se, just uncontrollable, and unruly. Their parents seem to think that all this manhandling is normal, but I don't. I hate it. How'd you like it if you were sleeping soundly one minute, then hit in the head with a plastic bat the next?

Gabby, I don't want to take matters into my own hands, but it may have to come to that. What should I do? I don't want to go back to the shelter, as homes for adult male chow chows don't come easily. Help!

Your (exhausted) admirer,

Abused in Amarillo

DEAR ABUSED,

These days, humans don't seem to discipline their puppies nearly as efficiently as we dogs do our own. Why? Not sure. Maybe they're scared of the hairless little goblins. In any event, parents often get a dog as a plaything for their kids, in hopes that the pet will amuse the tykes, and teach them something about animals. What they forget is that, like the kids, the dog has the right not to be abused, or harmed.

When puppies are still in the litter, they play hard, and often bite and bully each other. That's normal behavior for the little ones, who are developing their own little brat pack hierarchy, and learning proper social skills to boot. When one puppy bites another's ear too hard, the resulting scream or reprisal teaches the biter not to do it again.

Though an efficient method, it cannot be used on human children, because dogs simply cannot be allowed to bite, ever. Humans are just too vulnerable for that.

So, when kids act like aggressive, belligerent puppies, what's a dog to do? Ideally, our owners should take care of the situation, by teaching their kids how to properly interact with us. Unfortunately, they usually don't, and are often not even aware of what's going on until it's too late. When a three-year-old yanks on a dog's ear too hard and gets bitten, who do you think is going to end up in the shelter?

So, what should owners do to prevent this scenario? First, they should think long and hard about whether or not a dog will fit into their lifestyle. With several little children about, many parents simply won't have the time to properly raise and train a dog, which will need nearly as much attention as a human child (especially a puppy).

In my humble opinion, I think they should wait until their kids are a bit older, and in school. An eight-year-old can comprehend doggy do's and don'ts much easier than can a two-year-old, and can even help with the training and upkeep. If the parents think owning a dog might be too much work, why not get a low-maintenance pet, such as a fish or gerbil?

Then there is the issue of breed selection. If kids are around, parents should opt for a highly sociable, easy-going breed, and avoid those with less tolerance for the unexpected. Retrievers and retriever mixes typically make the best family pets, though standard poodles, shepherds, and collies also do well. Chow chows, Chinese shar-peis, Rottweilers, mastiffs, Lhasa apsos, great Pyrenees, and other territorial dogs bred for guard duty usually have a lower tolerance for kiddy abuse. There are exceptions to every rule, of course, but, in general, labs and goldens do best.

Once the decision to get a dog is made, parents should instruct their kids on which behaviors are appropriate, and which are not.

Under no circumstances should any pulling, tugging, yanking, or hitting ever be allowed! Only gentle touching and stroking should be permitted.

Next, the kids should learn how to walk the dog, and give it simple commands. Doing so will teach the pooch to respect and obey the children. Once this is established, dominant or aggressive gestures by the dog toward the kids will lessen, or disappear.

You're in a bad situation, pal, because of the abusive kids, and also because of your chow chow heritage. Let your owners see this letter before you take matters into your own mouth and end up in a desert junkyard in El Paso, okay? Good luck, bud.

Boundaries   Are   Vital

Dear Gabby,

I just got back from my third breakout.
This time, I made it all the way to the
interstate before the screws got me. Took
three of them, a dart gun, and a big net.
Next time I'm going at night, after dinner
and lights out.

Gab, I was born to run. A one-year-old
unneutered Siberian husky male, these
paws were made for running, and no fence,
door, window, or kennel can hold me. I
love my family, but these itchy feet have
got a hold of me like a pit bull on a
porterhouse.

I'm tied up in the garage right now,
but I figure two or three nights of howling should take care of that. Any suggestions on what to do if they try leg irons,
or duct tape?

Yours,

Roaming in Richmond

DEAR ROAMING,

Sounds like you need a sled and a one-way ticket to Alaska, blue eyes. Seriously, what's so bad about home? And where are your owners during these breakout attempts?

Some of us inevitably find a way out of the home or yard, and out into the busy streets. The escape is usually made through an open window, gate, or door, and less often, from an automobile. Sometimes a determined dog will dig under a fence to freedom. Dogs allowed to wander near home sometimes go too far, become disoriented, and end up lost.

We dogs are a curious bunch, with excellent senses that sometimes lead us astray. An open window or door, combined with the scent of a cat or another dog outside is often all it takes to lure one of us out into what may be a dangerous environment. Leave the front door open, and even the most timid dog is apt to investigate.

An unneutered dog is a prime candidate to make a "break" for it. A male dog can travel many miles in an attempt to mate. By the time he finds his perfect woman, he's miles from home. Unneutered females can also roam, though they typically won't travel as far.

Dogs whose owners move to new neighborhoods can become homesick for their old territories, and might decide to look for it. These dogs can search in vain for the old place, and become lost in the process.

A newly adopted shelter dog might try to escape within a few days of being adopted, in an attempt to find his old owners. It makes no difference how loving the new owners are; if the dog lived for many years with a previous owner, he may try to find his old home again.

Owners with poor control over their dogs often do not have the authority to command them to come back once off-leash and outside the home. If a dog does not recognize an owner's leadership, he will ignore all commands and go wherever he pleases.

Kids often do not have the strength to hold onto a dog's leash while on a walk. The dog may take off after another animal, or decide to go for an untethered stroll through the neighborhood. As children rarely have much authority over us, it becomes nearly impossible for them to call us back.

Then there are the tunneling experts. Dogs who dig often escape from yards or dog runs; left by themselves for much of the day, these tunnelers do so out of boredom, or from a desire to go after another animal. Terriers are famous for this type of escape.

You are definitely a hard case, Roamer. You are a husky, a breed known for its independent, roaming nature. Plus, you're unneutered. I don't know the rest of the

story, but I'm willing to bet that your people haven't obedience trained you, and haven't got a clue about establishing boundaries. Though you are a rebel and a gypsy, they have done nothing to curb your urge to escape. If they don't, you're going to end up kissing a bumper. You need to stop and smell the Alpo, dude, and learn how good home life can be. If you are interested, here are a few suggestions for your owners. Try to leave this letter where they can find it.

First, they need to check all possible escape routes out of the home and yard, making sure that you have no way out. If a window needs to be open, a secure screen without tears should be in place. The same goes for doors; if one needs to be open, a secure screen door should be in place. For a determined dog like you though, I'd keep the door closed entirely, as you would fly through a screen door.

Some dogs do not like car travel, and often become stressed by it; give them an out, and they will take it. If you're one of those, your owners can prevent this by putting you in a secure pet carrier whenever you travel.

If you spend time in a yard or dog run, your people should make sure the fence has no openings, and is high enough to prevent you from jumping over (in the case of a husky, that would have to be at least six feet). Also, they should consider having poured concrete or concrete blocks right up to the edge of the fence, to eliminate the possibility of your digging out. At the very least, the fence should have no openings along the ground. A one-foot-wide strip of chicken wire along the inner perimeter of the fence, covered with a thin layer of dirt and grass, or camouflaged with ivy, will also help.

Some companies now sell a product known as "invisible fencing." Installed underground, the system contains a dog within unseen boundaries by sending out an electronic warning to a sensor on the dog's collar. Though effective on many dogs, some territorial or independent breeds (like Rottweilers or you huskies) will blow right through the barrier to freedom. What works for a poodle won't necessarily work on you, Roam.

Children who leave windows or doors open allow dogs a tempting avenue out. If your owners have children, they should talk to them about closing all doors and windows, to prevent you from getting out.

Kids also often cannot hold onto a leash tight enough; if at the park or on the street, a dog like you could pull free. If the kids are strong enough, they should learn how to properly walk you. In your case, I wouldn't expect a child under the age of fourteen to have the strength to restrain you. After all, you dudes pull sleds.

Sorry to say, but having you neutered will minimize your desire to roam and mate. A castrated male won't seek out that female in heat a mile away, and a spayed female won't desire to seek out a mate.

Any new dog needs to be closely monitored for several months, and not allowed to be off-leash until properly obedience trained. Eventually, if trained and led well, he'll consider his new master worthy of loyalty and devotion.

An owner who fails to establish rules and leadership with his or her dog runs a higher risk of it escaping. For an owner like this, taking an obedience class and setting fair, firm rules are essential.

An owner should place an identification tag on his or her dog. Better yet, any veterinarian can install an identity microchip under a dog's skin, one that can be read by any shelter. This could save your life!

Lastly, a dog should be provided with an interesting environment to prevent boredom. Toys, chews, or anything else he finds appealing should be given to him. Trick and obedience training also help. By doing so, an owner can divert a wandering dog's energies back into his own territory, and away from thoughts of escape.

Roam, you've got to give up your traveling ways. Trust me; the road will break you. If you give family life a chance, you just might begin to appreciate what the little girl in the red shoes meant when she said, *"there's no place like home."*

Is There an Echo in Here?

Dear Gabby,

I'm a four-year-old male Jack Russell terrier with a strange problem. What does it mean when your owner repeats herself a dozen times? Is she going daft? I'm a bit worried about her, actually, and hope nothing's gone wrong.

It's been going on for a while now. She'll ask me to sit in this sweet, soppy voice that, honestly, a gerbil wouldn't take seriously. When I don't sit immediately, she keeps asking, over and over again, sometimes ten or fifteen times. Finally, to end the embarrassment, I sit and gaze up at the poor, frustrated soul.

She's had this weird, repetitive habit since I've known her, but lately it seems to be getting worse. I don't think she even knows she's doing it, Gabby; she just repeats herself over and over, until, out of pity, I do what she's asking me to do. About the only things she doesn't say a million times are the words *"Dinner"* and *"Cookies."* She says those only once. Strange, huh?

Gabby, I'd hate for anything bad to happen to her. Should I get her into the vet?

Your caring friend,
Concerned in Compton

DEAR CONCERNED,

Ah yes, the broken record syndrome. Sad, isn't it? Some owners just don't understand leadership rules. Let me explain what's going on here.

When a competent pack leader asks a subordinate to do something, the request is proffered once, and only once. That's all it should take to evoke the proper obedient response. Think an Alpha wolf has to ask ten times? Fat chance. If a subordinate blows off the desires of the Alpha, it gets disciplined immediately, and fairly. The subordinate quickly learns to take the Alpha seriously, and to respond the first time asked. This ensures that the pack will respond quickly to its leader during times of danger or need.

Unfortunately, your owner hasn't gotten the hang of this leadership thing. When she asks you to do something, it's done with no sense of confidence or competence. Instead of being a command, it becomes a sweet request, with no consequences for you should you decide to disobey. The annoying result of this is her asking you, time and time again, to perform the requested behavior. In effect, you have trained her to ask a dozen times instead of once. Pretty clever, you Jack Russells.

Here's the deal, Jack. One day, your owner is going to need you to respond quickly to a command, in order to ensure your safety. You might be chasing your ball out into the street as a Porsche bears down upon you. If you don't obey the *"Come"* command the very first time, they'll be scraping you off the grill. As it stands, it doesn't look good for you.

You need to learn to obey a command the first time asked. The first step in doing so is to have your owner ask once, and only once. If you choose to blow her off, some consequence (like a leash correction) must be experienced by you.

First, I'd suggest an obedience class for both of you. She needs to learn how to become a better leader, and you need to learn your place. Believe it or not, you're not supposed to be the leader!

Once she learns to develop a slightly more commanding presence and demeanor, it'll be time to work on the specific problem. She should clip your leash onto your collar, then, in a confident tone ask you to *"Sit,"* once and only once. If you do not *immediately* do so, she should give you a proper leash correction while simultaneously saying the word *"No."* Then, she should again ask you to *"Sit,"* one time. If you still refuse, it's the correction and *"No"* again. Then the command is again given, once. When you finally do decide to comply, she should praise you big time, and reward you with a treat. Eventually you'll figure out that, if you respond the first time, you'll get that positive reinforcement, and avoid the negative.

Sorry, pal, but it's for the best. Life will become safer and less stressful for both of you if you respect her as your leader, and if she learns to give commands once, and only once. Then you two can get a parrot, and reminisce.

Equipment: The Good, the Bad, and the Ugly

Dear Gabby,

I'm a big male mastiff who just got back from three days in the pokey. When my owner's leash snapped during a walk, I took off after a squirrel, and didn't stop until the sun went down. Almost got the darned rodent, but he scampered up into an oak tree at the last moment and escaped.

When I finally looked around for my owner, she was nowhere to be found. The Feds picked me up the next day, and locked me up with a crazy saluki mix who wouldn't shut his trap all night.

Because my collar fell off while I was jumping a fence, they had no way of getting hold of my people. It began to look as if I'd either get adopted by some stranger, or else given the sleepytime juice.

Luckily, my owners finally came for me. It was pretty emotional, Gab; everybody was crying and jumping around. They didn't have a leash or collar for me, so the Feds let them borrow a nylon lead to take me to the car. On the way

home, I ran around inside the van, overjoyed
to be back with my family.

Gabby, I just wanted to share this happy
ending with your readers. If any of you end up
lost and alone, don't give up hope; your family will save you!

Sincerely,

Grateful in Grand Rapids

DEAR GRATEFUL,

I am truly overjoyed at your happy ending, big guy. The Feds aren't that bad, really, and the food is pretty tasty. Unfortunately, your letter has brought up a number of issues regarding equipment, issues I feel need addressing.

First, it sounds like your owner was using a pretty flimsy leash. You're a big dude; your leash needs to be up to the task. When they replace it, make sure they get the strongest one available. Either thick leather or nylon will do, provided it has a heavy-duty clip on the end. Using a thin leash meant for a smaller dog is just asking for trouble in your case.

Next is the issue of your collar. That it broke while you were clearing a fence is probably a blessing, as it could have caught itself on the top and strangled you. However, your ID tag was on it; without that, the Feds weren't able to call your owners. Apart from purchasing a quality collar and ID tag (with your name, and your owner's telephone number), I would suggest they have an identification microchip injected under your skin (usually on the nape). Containing all relevant info on you, it can be easily scanned and read by shelters or veterinarians, allowing them to find your owners. Don't worry, it wouldn't hurt.

The other thing that struck me about your letter was the manner in which your family took you home. First, I think they should have bought a good leash and collar on the way to the shelter, to make absolutely sure you wouldn't get away again. A flimsy nylon lead just doesn't cut it for me. Also, it sounds as if they just let you wander around inside the van while they drive. This is dangerous, especially with a big happy dog like you. You could cause an accident by bumping into the driver. And, during a fender bender, you would go flying forward in the van, hurting yourself and others. Instead, they should have you ride inside an airline-approved pet carrier, in the back of the vehicle. By doing so, all of you would be safer. They use seat belts; why shouldn't you have some type of protection? At the very least, they could install a metal pet barrier in between you and the passenger compartment, to prevent you from interfering with the van's operation, and from flying forward during an accident.

The following is a brief summary of do's and don'ts regarding dog-related equipment. Show it to your owners, pal, so that they can more efficiently deal with the day-to-day issues of owning a dog.

Leashes:

Owners should always choose a leash strong enough to handle the weight and power of the dog in question. For dogs over forty pounds, a six-foot leash made of three-quarter-inch-thick leather or nylon is mandatory. Avoid chain leashes, as they are murder on human hands, and can break a

dog's teeth if chewed upon. For dogs weighing between twenty and forty pounds, a six-foot, half-inch-thick leash is sufficient. Dogs smaller than this can usually make do with a lighter-gauge leash. In any case, opt for a better-quality leash, with a strong clip at the end, preferably made of brass, or stainless steel. Don't go for the plastic, as these break. Regarding length, I recommend a six-foot leash for any dog, as it allows the owner to work on a wide variety of training exercises. A three- or four-foot leash is nearly worthless for this.

Collars:

Never skimp on a collar. Always buy the best available, made from either nylon or leather. Make sure an ID tag can be attached to it. Be sure it fits properly. For puppies, make sure it will adjust to the dog's growth. Never use a collar that's too big or too small.

Regarding training collars, the old slip collar, or "choke chain" works well, provided the owner has learned to use it in obedience class. It should be made of forged stainless steel, and not cast metal, to prevent breakage. Slip collars also come in nylon, if preferred. Be sure to use the proper size for your dog. If in doubt, consult the pet shop manager.

I usually steer owners away from the multipronged "pinch collars," as most do not know how to use them properly. Used only on a temporary basis with powerful, obstinate dogs, these medieval devices work best in the hands of a pro-

fessional trainer. If you think your dog needs one, odds are
you need help.

Recently a type of collar known as a "face collar" has
popped up. Working much like a bridle on a horse (without
the bit), the face collar attaches to the dog's head, and has a
ring that hangs down under the chin. Once the leash is
clipped to this ring, the owner can easily prevent the dog from
pulling. Control the head and you control the dog. Though
they work well, a very strong dog can pull out of one.

Electronic Training Devices:

Bark collars electronic remote trainers, available to help
owners end unwanted behaviors, should be used only after
consultation and instruction from a professional trainer. Owners should not purchase and use these potentially dangerous,
painful devices on their own, as they can do much more harm
than good. A professional trainer will recommend their use
only when no other training option is available. If you think
you need one, pick up the phone and call a trainer first.

Harnesses:

Some owners opt for using a harness instead of a collar.
Fitting about the dog's chest and shoulders, it has a ring on
top that a leash can clip to. My advice is to avoid them for
training purposes, as they simply do not offer any control.
Also, a big dog will pull you right down the street if wearing
a harness. Toy dogs do okay with harnesses, though, as their
delicate necks can be hurt by tension on a collar.

Pet Carriers:

Every dog should have its own pet carrier, or crate. I prefer the plastic type over the wire mesh, as it affords a certain feeling of privacy. The wire ones make me feel exposed, like a fish in a bowl. Owners should make sure that the crate they buy is airline approved, and big enough for the dog to stand and turn around in. Use it in the car, home, or hotel room.

Automatic Feeders:

A few companies sell gravity or electronically controlled automatic feeders, for dogs left alone for long periods. I used one once, and got fat as a hog. Though they work for some dogs, my advice to owners is to feed your dogs at specific times. Doing so allows you to tell exactly how much food is being eaten, and also allows you to create a "food drive" in your pet, which can then be used for training purposes. You shouldn't be leaving your dog alone for long periods anyway, so opt out of this one.

Cheap Stuff:

Never purchase cheap equipment. It breaks, and causes the potential for escape. When in doubt, spend more.

Like I said, make sure your owners get a look at this list—especially since it's time for them to head to the store to buy you new stuff. And I know it won't do any good to say this, but try a little harder to control yourself the next time you see a squirrel.

PART 3

The Right Way to Run the Home Environment

To a dog, there really is no place like home. It's our territory, and our base of operations. Our desire to love and protect the home turf is one reason humans love us so much. I've had more than a few, and loved each and every one.

It follows, then, that the way the home is set up and run is crucial to our happiness, right? After all, we spend most of our time there, eating, sleeping, and interacting. What goes on in the home affects us daily, and defines us as dogs.

Unfortunately, as the following letters will reveal, all is not well at the Ponderosa, boys and girls. Owners inadvertently make a myriad of errors in and around the home, errors which can cause behavior problems, or even threaten the safety of a dog.

In Part Three, I'll share some of the most pertinent ones with you dogs. Hopefully, you'll learn from them, and perhaps convince your owners to make whatever changes are necessary to assure your safety and happiness. Sit back, grab some chew, and read on!

All by Myself

Dear Gabby,

I've started barking to myself. My owner leaves me home all day, and by the afternoon I'm nutty. Lucky for him, I've got a big yard. Otherwise I'd be redecorating the house pretty well every day, if you get my drift.

Gabby, a two-year-old male Doberman shouldn't be barking to himself, should he? I mean, isn't that a sign of rabies or something? I spend the day eating dandelions and singing songs. Help.

Yours truly,

Abandoned in Albany

DEAR ABANDONED,

You're not crazy, pal, just isolated. Your owner must think you're a sheep or something.

This letter is similar to *Lonely in Las Vegas*'s, but with a bit more hope. That poor pooch didn't have a yard, and had no chance to relieve herself. You don't have that problem, but simply can't stand being cooped up back there all day with no interaction.

Your owner has several solutions to the problem. First, he can get another dog to keep you company back there. When he has a large fenced-in yard, taking care of two isn't a whole lot harder than caring for one, especially if he adopts a younger, smaller pooch. The new dog would amuse you, and give you someone to sing to.

The other solution is for your owner to have friends, neighbors, or a pet-sitting service come over once or twice during the day to play with you. Or, he could take a long lunch and do it himself. If opting for this, he would be able to keep you inside the home—for at least part of the day—where you might feel more at ease. That way, you'd also be able to protect the place.

He could even drop you off at a doggy day care a few times per week. Though it's a bit on the expensive side, you'd have plenty of company and lots to do.

At the very least, he could set a radio to an AM talk radio station, and play it through a window facing out toward the yard, to give you the feeling of companionship. Additionally, he could supply you with toys and chews, and perhaps some "enrichment" devices, such as a hard rubber toy with peanut butter smeared onto the inside of it. That'd keep you occupied, brother.

Show this letter to that absent landlord, pal. Maybe he'll get you a little friend, or at least do something to restore your sanity. Good luck, and beware of little voices.

Left Out in the Cold

Dear Gabby,

I'm dirty, cold, stressed, and bored, and I'm not going to take it anymore. This yard is no place for a well-bred pointer to be, let me tell you.

It's about twenty-five degrees right now, with an inch of snow on the ground. I'm shivering, and the water in my bowl is one big ice cube. I usually dig holes to pass the time, but the ground is too hard for that today, so I've been gnawing on the neighbor's picket fence and barking at crows.

Gabby, my owners parked me out here when I was a pup and, apart from a few quick visits into the house or garage, this is where I've been. Oh, sure, I sometimes go to the beach or on hunting trips, but other than that, it's these four fences for me.

I'd like to have some company every now and then, and maybe share the house with the rest of my pack, but they never let me inside. What should I do?

Your friend,

Caged in Kalamazoo

DEAR CAGED,

Sounds like you need an Old English sheepdog to cuddle up with. Seriously, many owners fall into the trap of leaving their pooches outside for long stretches of the day, with some actually parking their poor dogs out there 24/7. Some of them think that a dog prefers to be outside in "nature," while others, unable to properly housetrain or control their pets, resort to containing the pooch in the yard or a pen for inordinate periods of time.

Unfortunately, several bad things happen when owners choose this option. You dogs in question never really become housetrained, because you can relieve yourself anytime and anywhere you want. You never learn to "hold it." You also never learn proper house manners, and tend to become somewhat antisocial due to your lack of contact with people or other pets.

Yard or pen dogs often bark or dig incessantly, and can become dirty and infested with parasites. You guys sometimes escape, resulting in your getting lost or injured.

With shorthaired or toy breeds, an outdoor life sentence can also result in illness or death from the elements. At the very least, you outdoor dogs usually develop joint disorders sooner than your indoor counterparts.

Why do your owners keep you out there? My hunch is that, when they first got you, they quickly realized that your high level of activity (pointer, right?) made you difficult to control indoors. Worried about what you might do to the furnishings, rug, etc., they stuck you outside. Once there, you became even more hyper and a bit stinky, if I might venture a guess. What person wants a high-strung, dirty dog in his or her home? Your nonexistent potty training closed the deal; you became an outdoor dog for the duration.

Here's what you need to do, pal. First, stop barking at the crows; they're stupid and evil and unimportant. Second, sneak into the home and leave this reply in the bathroom, where they're sure to find it.

They need to start from the beginning with you; basic obedience training comes first, to ensure control. Next, have them buy a sturdy plastic travel crate, to be kept somewhere in the home. When you aren't being supervised, you need to be in it to prevent any "accidents" indoors. They need to feed you and take you outside on a precise schedule, to teach you the basics about housetraining; the crate will be an invaluable part of this switchover in that it will prevent destruction to the home, and teach you to "hold it."

Slowly, they will be able to give you more and more freedom indoors, until you can be left alone for periods of time without supervision. Why should they do this? First, the home is the "den" of the pack; you will feel as if you belong again. This

will reduce your stress and help resocialize you. Second, you will be warm and parasite-free, possibly for the first time in your life. Third, you will be able to protect the home, and warn of any possible break-ins with that well-practiced bark of yours.

If they aren't home for eight or more hours at a time, they can have a friend or neighbor come by to let you out, or else hire a pet walker to come by once a day. If that's not an option, they can keep you in the yard while they are at work and then bring you inside when they get home. It will take some patience and work on their part (and on yours), but this can be done!

Good luck, pal; I know how lonely and boring the yard can be. Take my advice, though, and quit munching the neighbor's fence, as wood can make potty time a rather piercing experience.

All Tied Up

Dear Gabby,

I'm a three-year-old German shepherd female dragging 20 feet of chain around a cruddy old yard. My owners used to let me roam around the entire yard until I dug out and took off for the next county last month. Now they have me on this chain, attached to a big metal post in the center of the yard. I just go round and round and round . . . you know the drill.

Gabby, I'm going bananas back here. They do let me into the house when they come home, but in the meantime, it's a bit dizzying. Yesterday a squirrel pranced around the yard, then sat just out of range while he chewed open a chestnut. So close . . . so close. The only upside of this whole mess is that all this dragging and pulling is making me strong as an ox. Should I accept my fate, or just yank out that darned post and head for the hills?

Yours truly,

Shackled in Cheboygan

DEAR SHACKLED,

I remember being on the "chain gang" once too, a long time ago. My first owners had me on a 20-foot cable in the front yard; every afternoon the kids walking home from school would razz me until I started barking my head off. After a year of it, I finally broke my collar and ran for the hills. I'll never forget those little rats walking by, though. Those faces—burned into my brain . . . never forget—never forget. . . .

Sorry about that. So, the old chain technique, huh? Grass worn away in a 40-foot circle? Links all rusted? Don't you hate when you get to the end of it and it stops you dead in your tracks, while that nasty little squirrel or cat is just two feet away, smirking at you? *Grrr!*

This letter is similar to the previous one *(Caged in Kalamazoo)*, with an added twist: Your movements are severely limited by the chain. You escaped from the yard once, so they've decided to keep you around by tethering you. Well, nothing drives a dog crazier than limiting its movement in such a way. You can still see all of the distractions (squirrels, neighbors, birds, etc.), but can't do anything about them. Very frustrating! Plus, the physical restraint itself adds to your stress levels. When that chain stops your forward motion, you could just howl, right? That stresses you out, and makes you paranoid, right? "They" can get to you, but you can't get to them. For a German shepherd especially, this is torture.

Tethering a dog in a yard all day is dumb. It can turn a well-adjusted dog into an antisocial, fearful, aggressive misfit in no time. How would owners like it if they were limited to a 40-foot circle of land, while clowns and mimes and aluminum siding salespersons loitered just out of reach?

The only justification for tethering a dog is if you are a danger to others, and need to be restrained. If you're a dog who has gotten to this stage, however, you need the help of a trained canine behaviorist, and not 30 pounds of steel.

Get your owner to read this, as well as the previous letter. You need to get off the chain, and into the home. If they don't have the time to take care of you properly, they should give you to someone who can. Tell them to get a cat, for Pete's sake. Can you imagine one of THEM on a chain? Hah! They'd explode!

Stuck in a Truck

Dear Gabby,

Have you ever been to Texas in July? Hot enough to fry a frog on the dashboard of a pickup. Well, as a toy poodle, I'm not much bigger than that frog, and I'm starting to sizzle.

My owner (bless her soul, 78 and still kicking) takes me with her to the market every other day. Likes my company, and the way I sit on her lap while she drives, with my paws up on the wheel of the old Plymouth. Anyway, the store won't let me come in with her, so I stay in the Plymouth and look after it while she walks the aisles.

Problem is, this time of year the old car gets as hot as a blast furnace in about five minutes. She leaves the windows cracked, but it doesn't make much of a difference. By the time she gets back, it's about 110 degrees, and my paws are sticking to the vinyl.

Gabby, last week a customer called a cop on the old gal, because it looked like I was done for. Truth was I did feel kind of faint that day, and couldn't pant fast enough to keep cool. I love going on trips with her, but don't think I can survive another scorcher like that. What should I do?

Yours very truly,
Fried in Fort Worth

DEAR FRIED,

Pan-fried poodle, eh? Sorry; this is serious business, so let me deal with it as such.

Hundreds of dogs die each year inside of overheated cars while their owners go about their chores, unaware of the crisis. Sure that the time spent away from the dog won't be harmful, they come back to find the pet prostrate, dead, or in the hands of a good Samaritan or police officer.

Heat kills. Dogs (especially little guys like you) don't have the same ability to cool themselves off that people do. We lack sweat glands, and can only pant to rid ourselves of excess heat. Plus, we have a fur coat on, all of the time!

Little dogs are even worse off, because their smaller bodies contain less water than their larger counterparts, and therefore dehydrate and heat up more quickly. Put a toy breed into a closed car in the heat of a Texas summer, and you've got a fricassee in the making.

I'm surprised at the ignorance of your owner, pal. Did she just relocate from Fairbanks?

Let me set down a few basic rules for this situation. First, owners should *never* leave a dog inside a car for *any length of time* once temperatures rise above 70 degrees, period. With the windows closed, a car quickly becomes an oven, killing a dog in short order.

Keeping a window or two cracked won't do much, either, except to prolong the inevitable (or give a thief a great head start). If your goofy owner doesn't believe it, have her sit in the car for an hour with the windows closed and a thermometer in her sweaty little hand.

Below 70 degrees, a dog can be kept in a car (with several windows cracked open at least a few inches) for up to 15 minutes maximum, no more. People have to understand that a dog's ability to cool itself doesn't come close to matching their own: What seems tolerable to humans can be unbearable to a pooch.

Most dogs should be able to tolerate being in a car for up to an hour when temperatures range from 40 to 50 degrees, provided a window is cracked open for air circulation. Any lower than that, however, and small dogs (and those with short coats) could eventually suffer hypothermia.

The best advice I can give your owner is for her to leave you home in the nice air-conditioned house while she does her shopping. She'll survive the separation, and so will you, I'm sure. At least have her wait until November or December, when temperatures in your neck of the woods drop to survivable levels.

If she still insists on taking you along in that pressure cooker of a Plymouth, maybe you can change her mind by leaving a few choice "gifts" on her seat each time she leaves you to roast. Bet *that* will change her behavior right quick, partner!

Where's *My* Seat Belt?

Dear Gabby,

I'm a big male chocolate lab who loves riding in the back of my owner's pickup. Well, at least up until last week, that is, when we had a bit of an accident. Some birdbrain ran a red light, causing my owner to jam on the brakes. I went crashing into the back of the cab. Next thing I know, I'm at the vet's office with tubes down my throat and a Chihuahua-size lump on my noggin.

Gabby, is there anything I can do to stop knucklehead humans from driving like maniacs? Luckily, my owner had his seatbelt on and didn't get hurt (thank goodness!). Any advice you can give me on this one will be greatly appreciated.

Your fan,

Bruised in Buffalo

DEAR BRUISED,

I'm not sure how many knuckleheads we actually have in this story. Listen, Bruised; your problem isn't so much the crazies running red lights as it is the goofball driving your truck. Know why you got hurt and he didn't? Come on; get that retriever brain humming, pal. You said it yourself: *He had his seat belt on!* What did you have protecting you? A bed liner and a tailgate?

Listen up, pilgrim; your life is just as important as his, right? At least to you, that is. So then, why shouldn't *you* have some way of protecting yourself in the event of an accident, just as he does? They've got seat belts, front and side air bags, ABS brakes, and a bunch of other fancy doodads to keep them safe. Why shouldn't you?

In my opinion, every dog that rides in a car or truck should either be in an airline-approved travel crate, or in a harness that attaches to one of the seat belts inside the vehicle. Those are the only ways to reliably ensure the safety of a pooch in a crash. Otherwise, you'll get tossed around violently, risking serious injury or death. If unsecured inside the car, your flailing body could even hurt or kill the driver, or others.

By allowing you to ride in the back of the truck, your owner needlessly risked your life. He's regretting it now though, emotionally and financially. While it looks cool, a dog in the back of a pickup is a tragedy waiting to happen.

Here's what you need to do. First, get that cowboy owner of yours to buy you a sturdy plastic travel crate, and then firmly secure it down to the front of the truck bed, either by using tie-downs or by bolting it right to the bed. Then, have him put you in there whenever the two of you go cruising. If you get into an accident again, the crate will restrain your movement, and keep you from flying out the back.

If he doesn't like that idea, have him buy you a dog harness at the pet store, the kind that allows for the passenger seat belt to slip through it. That will at least prevent you from crashing through the window and cutting yourself to ribbons. Some harnesses will even adapt to the bed of a pickup, allowing your owner to secure you back there by means of a series of cables. Though this method isn't as safe as a crate, it's better than nothing.

If your owner has a car (or room inside of a truck), a crate secured on a back seat or in the storage area will work well to protect you from injury, and also keep you from becoming a deadly projectile. An added bonus of this method is that the crate can prevent a destructive dog from chewing the upholstery to shreds. (It sounds like you're not that kinda guy, though.)

Your owner needs to get a clue and stop taking *your* life into his own hands. Got that, Bruised?

Ignoring the Pack Order

Dear Gabby,

For ten years they were happy with me. Everything was great. I fetched, shook hands, came when called. Then *it* came. The doody geyser, the heir apparent, the prince. Seems that my owners weren't satisfied with this old male mutt anymore, and decided to buy a pure-bred golden retriever puppy to liven things up a bit.

Well, Gabby, things are pretty live, let me tell you. The little bastard runs around like a jack rabbit, getting into everything. He eats my food, sleeps on my bed, and tries to pull his baby macho games on me. *Me.* He's even started marking over my spots. Is nothing sacred anymore?

Here's the problem, Gab. Every time I try to put the little stinker in his place, my owners come down on me like distemper. When I growl at him for nosing into my dish, they yell at me. When he steals my favorite ball and I body slam him for it, they lock me in my crate for an hour. Yesterday, he growled at *me,* and they laughed and said it was cute. Excuse me, but when did this suddenly become a democracy?

Gabby, I'm either going to eat him or run away. What's your advice?

Regrettably,
Disregarded in Duluth

DEAR DISSED,

Next thing you know these puppies will get the vote. Honestly, I sympathize with you, dude. Nothing is more annoying than an impertinent child running amok, without guidance or direction from the owners.

The reason you are having this problem is (you guessed it) the ignorance of your owners. They do not understand the mechanics of the pack hierarchy, and how it is crucial for the dogs in the home to work out their pecking order on their own. Barring outright aggression (which rarely happens), you should have the right to put the little poop in his place. It's actually good for him, as it will teach him to respect those who could potentially hurt him. As it is now, he might storm up to some strange Rottweiler at the park and get his little clock cleaned.

Owners think that everyone should get along in democratic harmony, including dogs. In their minds, all dogs are created equal. A worthy ideal, but completely bogus in our world. Without a pecking order there would be chaos. When they punish you for trying to put the puppy in his place, they are actually doing him a disservice. He isn't learning to respect or obey those in a position of authority over him, and will undoubtedly get into trouble sometime soon. They don't understand that as the elder, dominant dog, you can actually make their job much easier, by teaching the little punk to obey without delay.

Let those utopians you live with read this, Dissed. Then maybe they will allow you to teach the pup how to respect the pecking order.

Here are some rules that owners should abide by when bringing a new puppy into a home with a resident dog. If they read these, things should begin to improve:

1. The puppy shouldn't mess with the established dog's food, toys, or bed.
2. He should be fed after the dominant dog.
3. The dominant dog should not be punished for growling at or disciplining the puppy if he breaks any of the above rules (unless it gets out of hand).
4. The dominant, established dog should be greeted and petted first.
5. The dominant dog should be allowed to sleep higher up, and go through doors first.
6. If the puppy growls at the dominant dog, let them work out the conflict between themselves.
7. Only interfere if full-blown aggression occurs (but do not separate two fighting dogs—use a hose or a glass of water instead).

If the new dog does eventually become the domi-nant pooch in the home,

however, the same rules should apply; it should be allowed to discipline the other dog(s) when necessary.

Listen, Dissed: Don't hurt the little punk, but do what you gotta do, you know what I'm saying to you? In the long run, you'll be doing him a favor.

Born Free?

Dear Gabby,

Yesterday I got smacked in the butt by a car while roaming the hood. Nothing serious, but it shook me up pretty badly, and gave me a sore rump.

Here's my question: I love visiting my buddies down the street, but am now leery of all that morning traffic. Is this some sort of post-traumatic stress thing? Do I need to see a shrink? Will I get over it? I hope so, because there's a new cat that moved in a few blocks down the road, and I'm planning on a little housewarming party for him. What's your advice?

Your friend,

Woozy in Worcester

DEAR WOOZY,

You don't need a shrink; you need a leash. Your owners need the shrink. What are they thinking, letting you wander the streets? This isn't 1823, and you aren't a superhero impervious to 4,000-pound killing machines zooming down the road at 60 miles per hour.

Let's face it: We're not on the farm anymore, and our owners don't travel in horse-drawn carts. Neighborhoods are crisscrossed with roads, fences, highways, train tracks, and all manner of obstructions and dangers. I don't care how street savvy you think you are, pal; sooner or later you'll get nailed but good.

Your owners don't let their kids play in traffic, do they? So why should they let you? If you want to exercise and see the sights, let them clip a leash onto your collar and walk you around.

No dog is smart enough or fast enough to forever avoid injury in this automobile-dominated, fast-paced world. Unless you live on 30 acres in the middle of nowhere, it's best to stay on your own property, and leave the roaming to the alley cats.

There are plenty of ways for you to have fun without prancing down the double yellow. Here are a few:

1. Schedule a play date at the doggy park, where you and your buddies can run around to your heart's content.

2. Play a nice game of fetch in the fenced yard.
3. Go for a long walk with your owners.
4. Take a tricks or agility class at a local canine training facility.
5. Go for a swim.
6. Have a doggy friend come over to your home and hang out in the yard.
7. Talk your owners into getting a second dog.

To prevent you from escaping and taking off, they should be sure to have a sturdy fence, one too high for you to jump over. Doors to the home should be closed firmly; if only the screen door is closed, they need to lock it. Windows should be closed, too, or at least properly screened. And all kids in the home must heed the closed door and window policy!

To be on the safe side, you should have an identification tag on your collar, with their telephone number on it, as well as your name. Additionally, your vet can inject an identification chip beneath your skin, which can be easily scanned to reveal all your vital info.

Got it? Good! Now show this letter to your nutty owners before I come over there and bump all of your heads together.

Bored Brainless!

Dear Gabby,

I'm writing to get advice on my situation. A two-year-old female beagle, I got in big trouble last week for ripping up the sofa, and for digging into the potted plants. Last month, my owners stuck a bark collar on me, because I'd begun howling during the day. Just a few minutes ago, I broke into the trash and spread it all around the house.

Gabby, am I going crazy? I just can't seem to behave myself during the day when my owners are at work. It's like another dog takes over and forces me to do things I know I shouldn't be doing. I'm even licking and chewing on my own feet, causing nasty sores to erupt. Why can't I just be happy to lie around the house and sleep?

A big fan,

Destructive in Dayton

DEAR DESTRUCTIVE,

Relax. You're not suffering from multiple personalities, or possessed by demons. The problem here is (can you guess?) your owners. For some inexplicable reason, they have decided to leave a young beagle home alone, without a thing to do all day. Talk about asking for trouble—I'm surprised you haven't burned the place down by now.

Dogs need stimuli in their lives, just like people. Without it, we go bananas. Now, in my letter called "Don't Forget to Learn Your Tricks!" I suggested to Humdrum, an Australian shepherd, that she have her owners teach her some tricks in order to satisfy her need for physical and intellectual challenges. In your case, I think it's your environment that needs modification.

Let me guess: You're alone for nine hours each day, with no other pets to keep you company, right? With nothing to do or see, you have begun to invent activities to pass the time and release stress. Tearing the sofa to shreds wouldn't have been my first choice, though, nor would licking craters into my feet. I probably would have made a break for it and rode the rails down to New Orleans, but hey, that's me.

What if you had things in the home to occupy your time? A hollow rubber chew toy with peanut butter smeared inside of it, maybe? Or small cookies left randomly about the home for you to find in your travels? How about a radio left on a talk radio station? These are just a few environmental enrichment techniques your owners could use to liven things up a bit for you while they are at work. Doing that would make for a more interesting, stimulating home environment, and minimize the chances of your becoming destructive and nutso.

Here's a list of things they can try to do to relieve your boredom:

1. Hard rubber chew toy or short length of PVC pipe with peanut butter smeared on the inside
2. Television or radio left on a talk or news station
3. Random placement of small treats throughout the home
4. Doggy door giving access to a fenced yard or dog run
5. Surprise visit by a friend or neighbor
6. The playing of a 30-second endless-loop audio tape, with an owner's happy voice on it
7. The placement of olfactory stimuli, or "aroma therapy," such as sprinkled cinnamon and allspice, instant soup mixes, bouillon cubes, ever-green boughs, coffee grounds, or rum or vanilla extract

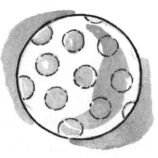

8. Random relocation of food and water dishes

9. Frozen cubes of broth with meat inside

10. Raw egg, with the shell still intact, left in the dog's food dish

11. Unbreakable mirrors, placed low

12. Dog crate with cozy blanket inside

13. Additional pets

14. Temperature variations, or changes in lighting

15. Changes in flooring materials, e.g., the placement of area rugs onto hardwood floors

16. Random placement of vet-approved toys and chews

17. Random phone calls home, with the owner leaving an audible message on the answering machine

18. Hair cuttings or feathers from another animal left in strategic places in the home

19. Occasional rearrangement of furniture

20. Aquariums (with a top securely fastened)

If your owners implemented some of these environmental techniques for you, don't you think you would have a better time of it? I know I would! Leave this letter out for them, pal; odds are they'll get a clue and make your environment a more stimulating one. In doing so, they'll end up holding onto their new sofa for a good long time.

A Plea for Doggy-Proofing

Dear Gabby,

Please excuse the veterinary station-ary, as I am writing you from intensive care. Three days ago I discovered a big box of chocolates on the coffee table; needless to say, it didn't last long. Delicious, but, as I have learned, also quite deadly. Being an 80-pound big shepherd mix probably saved my life, as there wasn't quite enough poison in the candy to kill me outright. I'm plenty sick though, and not out of the woods yet. I hate to think what would have happened to my Pekingese buddy down the street if he had gotten into that yummy box of death.

Gabby, why do people make bad things taste so good? Are they trying to kill us, or themselves? Enlighten me.

Still kicking,

Ailing in Altoona

DEAR AILING,

Whew! Close call, huh, partner? Let me say it right now; chocolate is poison to dogs and cats! Some chemical called *theobromine,* I think. Kills us, but not people. Sounds like a conspiracy to me, but what do I know?

Glad to hear you're going to pull through, pal. I can't tell you how many dogs die each year because of eating some toxic substance in the home. Drain cleaners, chocolate, bleach, antifreeze—you name it, a hundred things can lay low a dog in a heartbeat. If it is accessible, an unknowing puppy or adult dog can fall victim to it just like that.

In addition to imbibing poisonous substances, an overly curious dog might chew on an electrical wire, fall out of an open window, or escape through a screen door. Even ordinary houseplants can be harmful.

Any responsible dog owner should go through his or her home from stem to stern, in order to ensure that it is safe for a pet. For instance, an innocent little houseplant such as a dieffenbachia can be fatal to a small dog, if he decides to eat enough of it.

The following is a list of special areas, objects, and situations that your owners need to address in order to prevent a potentially fatal accident from occurring again. Show them this, Ailing, if you want to see your golden years:

1. Keep doors and windows closed, unless sturdy screens are in place. Remember though, that a strong dog can blow right through a screen.
2. The home is filled with substances that can hurt or kill a dog, including:

◆ Antifreeze
◆ Acids
◆ Acetaminophen, aspirin, or ibuprofen
◆ Alcohol
◆ Chlorine bleach
◆ Drain cleaner
◆ Fertilizer
◆ Gasoline or diesel fuel
◆ Household cleaners such as Windex, Lysol, or Mr. Clean
◆ Insecticides
◆ Motor oil
◆ Paint
◆ Prescription drugs
◆ Solvents such as paint thinner, rust remover, or tarnish remover
◆ Rat poison

These substances should be placed out of a dog's environment and behind securely locked cupboards, preferably located high up in the garage.

3. Oil spills, particularly those on the driveway, in the garage, or on the street, should be cleaned up, as contact with oil can make a dog ill. Above all, *no antifreeze can be left on the floor, driveway, or street,* as it is highly toxic, and can kill. Antifreeze has a sweet taste, so beware!

4. Owners should install childproof locks on all cupboards and drawers containing any potentially toxic substances.

5. Many house and garden plants are toxic to dogs. Owners should keep their dogs away from these, especially if the pooches have a penchant for nibbling on greenery. These include:

- Azalea
- Bean plants
- Cactus
- Crocus
- Daffodil
- Dieffenbachia
- Hemlock
- Hydrangea
- Ivy
- Lily
- Mistletoe
- Mushroom

- Narcissus
- Nightshade
- Oleander
- Philodendron
- Poinsettia
- Potato leaves
- Rhododendron
- Tobacco
- Tomato leaves
- Walnuts
- Yew

6. Owners should conceal power cords and wires to prevent us dogs from chewing on them and being electrocuted. Wires can be placed under carpets, or tacked beneath moldings along the floor.

7. Lastly, a concerned owner should install baby guard wall socket plugs into all unused electric wall sockets. Doing so will prevent a curious paw from reaching in and getting a shocking surprise.

I know this sounds like a lot, but convincing your owner to address these issues correctly might one day save your skin, pal. Feel better, and stay away from the sweets.

I Chew, Therefore I Am

Dear Gabby,

Yesterday I got into hot water for chewing to bits my owner's TV remote control. What can I say? I was bored, and it tasted good. Last month, his brown loafers ended up in my belly, as did his dress belt. Hey, if he's going to leave these things out, don't I have dibs on them?

Gabby, I like to chew. It helps pass the time, and besides, I'm teething, and the gnawing helps relieve the pain. But my owner likes television, and grumbles now each time he has to get up to change the channels. How can I avoid getting into trouble, but still satisfy my urge to chew?

Sincerely,

Chomping in Chicago

DEAR CHOMPING,

Contrary to popular belief, television is now man's (and woman's) best friend. We come in a distant second, I think.

Nothing is more upsetting to an owner than coming home to find the remote control in pieces on the carpet, or a good pair of shoes chewed to ribbons. These things have value to them, pal; by destroying them, you can get into big trouble.

That said, often it is the owner's fault. Too frequently they don't give us acceptable chewing alternatives. Let's face it: We love to gnaw, especially if we are teething. A good piece of leather can hit the spot, in my book.

They can prevent the destruction of valuable items pretty easily, though. Here's how:

1. Owners should dog-proof the home by picking up all vulnerable items such as shoes, belts, TV or VCR remotes, or anything else that is valuable to them.

2. You should then be given several chew toys of your very own, and be encouraged to chew on them. Nylon or rubber bones are preferable to rawhide or leather-type toys, simply because they are less similar to your owner's own leather items. Giving you leather products to chew on might encourage you to think that chewing on shoes and belts is also okay.

3. A puppy should not have access to the entire home when its owner is gone; this is an open invitation to disaster. Little ones are naturally curious, and will explore the home until something good to chew is found, usually a treasured possession of its master. Instead, a puppy should be kept in one room that has been "puppy-proofed," and provided with several chew toys to pass the time.

4. If a dog likes to chew on furniture or wooden moldings, its owner should go to the nearest pet shop and purchase an antichewing spray or paste, which can be applied to anything off-limits to the pooch. These sprays or pastes are made to have a very bitter taste, something we hate. If caught in the act, we should be reprimanded with a stiff *"No, Leave it!"* and perhaps a leash correction.

5. While a dog is learning proper chewing etiquette, it's probably a good idea for the owner to keep a short leash on the pet, in the home. This will allow him or her to correct the dog immediately upon some transgression.

Whatever methods your owner chooses, be sure he or she uses them consistently for at least six weeks, as that is how long it takes to effectively modify us dogs' bad behavior. Good luck. Hey, maybe he can train you to change the channels!

PART 4

Our Beloved Owners

CAN'T LIVE WITH 'EM,
CAN'T LIVE WITHOUT 'EM

L et's face it. We're stuck with them. There's no getting around it. As naïve to canine instincts as they sometimes are, people are essential to our well-being. They give us food, shelter, and love—three things no dog can live without.

Oh sure, we could roam the streets eating vermin and trash, but who wants to live like a cat? No; since the first time a bone was tossed onto the trash pile, dogs have had an inextricable bond with human beings.

That said, there's much that those two-leggeds still don't understand about us, and about the relationship. The letters in Part Four deal with this tenuous issue, so read carefully. Maybe you doggies out there will pick up a tip or two that might make life with the "hairless ones" a little easier, so get comfy and read on!

Praise Unearned Is Praise Unwanted

Dear Gabby,

My owner is a nitwit. Nothing the new puppy does is wrong. Nothing. When it's near her, she loves on it, even if it's not doing a thing. The little dirt bag could be drooling into his dish, and she'd praise it. When I was his age, I had to go to obedience school and earn my rewards the hard way.

Yesterday it ran off with my tennis ball. *My* tennis ball. Think it got in trouble? Not a chance. My owner praised the little tick bag! But when I tried to get the ball back, I got yelled at. People are insane. Insane!

Gabby, should she be praising this puppy all of the time, for no reason at all? The punk is becoming a spoiled little sissy, and I'm close to packing a grip and hitting the road. Any advice?

Yours desperately,

Old-Fashioned in Framingham

DEAR OLD-FASHIONED,

Hey, I'm old school too. I think a dog has to earn praise, and not just get it because of a cute mug.

Unfortunately, dog owners are famous for spoiling their pets. Who can resist the cute eyes of an eight-week-old puppy? Not many. Owners love them, and are willing to do anything in return for their love and attention. After all, that's why they get pets in the first place.

When owners begin giving their dogs unearned treats and attention, though, they set into motion a pattern of pushy, controlling behavior. We dogs quickly understand that, whenever we want, we can get an uninformed owner to give us food or attention, just with a bat of our eyes. Once a dog learns this, it begins to take charge of the pet/owner relationship. When this happens, a spoiled, pushy pet is born.

It starts simply enough. The puppy ambles over to your owner, who immediately pets it and coos over it. What does this puppy learn? It learns that it can demand attention from the owner whenever it wants, just by being there.

People think this is simply a loving interaction, but we dogs know better. It's really a power play; the puppy begins to realize that it has power over the owner, and can affect his or her behavior whenever it wants.

Owners who give unearned praise to their pets all day long are doing so because *they derive pleasure from the giving.* What a refreshing thing for the owner: to have an intelligent living thing pay immediate attention to him or her! In the end, though, unearned praise must be seen as an attention-getting ploy designed to raise the dog's status, and gain control.

If your owner continues to praise the puppy for no particular reason, and also fails to correct inappropriate behaviors, the little hairball will eventually become a spoiled brat. Instead of giving gratis praise, your hapless owner should instead praise and reward the dog *only when it has done something desirable,* like "sit" or "wait" or "shake." The puppy then becomes responsive to the owner's actions, and not vice versa.

In other words, praise or treats should be given only as a reward for the pet performing a desired task, or acting in a desirable manner. They should be *earned.* Attention should not be given simply because the pet is in the room. That is a recipe for pushy, dominant behavior.

Owners who disregard this advice are unknowingly spoiling their pets in an attempt to secure their love and attention. The point is: a competent, caring, confident owner does not need to *buy* a pet's love; it will be given freely, with no bribes needed, once the pooch knows who is in charge. By praising only when a dog acts responsibly, an owner shapes that pet's mindset for years to come.

Good luck, pal; maybe if they read this, things will get better. You might also try showing off some of your old obedience training; if you do, they might decide to send the little tyrant off to school, too.

Begging Embarrasses Us All

Dear Gabby,

I'm a six-year-old collie mix who was just recently adopted by a nice family in the suburbs. Everything seemed to be going fine until yesterday, when I sat next to the dinner table and begged for scraps--which is what I'd done for years with my previous owners. Well, to my surprise, they frowned, then put me in the basement for the rest of their meal!

Today I tried the begging routine at breakfast and lunch, with the same results. I don't much like the basement: How do I get out of there and get back to munching on some of those tasty handouts?

Hungrily yours,

Denied in Dubuque

DEAR DENIED,

Party's over, huh, pal? Sorry, but in this instance, your new owners are dead right. A dog who makes a pest out of himself at the dinner table can become a pushy, spoiled brat; better to look for food in your bowl.

The most common cause of begging behavior in a dog comes from the actions of the owner, who may have gotten into the habit of too often giving out pet treats and leftovers throughout the day. By doing so, well-meaning owners condition their pets to beg. In combination with this, the owner of a begging dog often has poor control over the pet, often a dominant animal with enough smarts to learn how to train its owner into giving it tasty tidbits whenever it wants them.

Unknowingly, the owner who does so loses more and more pack status, until he or she is plainly viewed as a subordinate. The dog enjoys a sense of power, and gets fat in the process.

You had it pretty good in your old home, pal. But I think these people have got your number. Get with the program, and let them eat in peace.

For other owners who might happen to read this letter, here are a few guidelines to follow regarding a begging pooch:

◆ Make sure your pet is at a proper weight, to ensure it is getting enough food.

- Feed it on a schedule, instead of free-feeding it all day. By doing so, you will teach it to expect food at a prescribed time, instead of any time it pleases. Its hunger will peak at feeding time instead of at random times during the day. Eventually, your dog will realize that food is no longer available any time it wants.

- Give a dog treats only when a particular behavior is being encouraged. If fed random treats throughout the day, a dog will learn to beg for more whenever it feels the desire.

- Never feed a dog food from the dinner table. Also, do not feed it food intended for human consumption. A dog who eats the same food a person does will assume it has equal status. Dog food only (whatever type that may be).

- Everything an owner does with his or her dog should teach it that, though loved, it is below people in the pecking order. Remember to be the boss!

- Never give a dog food while preparing a meal at the kitchen counter. Instead, place it in its food dish, at the prescribed doggy dinner time.

If, in an effort to beg, a dog jumps onto a person, a quick spritz of water from a plant sprayer bottle—right

in the mouth while saying "No!"—will stop that behavior in its tracks. Also, instruct other humans not to give the pet any treats, unless it is being trained to perform a specific, desirable behavior, such as "Sit" or "Come."

Sorry, Denied, if it seems like I'm giving the humans more advice than you. But the way I see it, when human and dogs are both aware of how the pecking order should work, everyone's happier in the long run.

Good luck, bud. And lay off the begging. It's embarrassing and unnecessary!

Hellos and Good-byes: Take It Easy!

Dear Gabby,

My owner is turning me into a nervous wreck. Each time she gets ready to leave the house, she gets all gushy and emotional, and acts like we'll never see each other again. "Oh, Sage, I'm going to miss you sooo much, honey . . . you'll be okay while I'm gone, right? Don't worry, though, I'll be back real soon, and then we can go to the park! Now give me a kiss, snookums!" Ugh. Can you say "over the top"? She's so melodramatic, I'm starting to think she knows something I don't. Is a meteor due to strike the planet? People been breaking into houses and eating lab mixes?

Her return home is just as stressful. "Sage! I'm hoooome! Come here, honey, and give me a big smooch! Come on, babe, chase me around the house! Yay!" Can anyone say "gag me"?

Gabby, she's great and all, but I can't take her energy anymore. Is there any way for me to get her to chill?

Stressfully,
Hyped Up in Helena

DEAR HYPED,

Don't tell me: No kids in the home, right? No spouse either? Just the two of you? Thought so. You're the only game in town, pal, the sole repository for that big well of love. I suppose it could be worse, but . . .

Owners who make a big deal out of greetings and departures do their pooches a big disservice. When your owner gets you all worked up that way, it can cause you to become hyperactive, stressed, and mindless (as in, losing your mind . . .).

Any dog lacking in confidence can also develop separation anxiety because of this bizarre owner habit. Upon seeing its owner go into his or her frenetic "departure ritual," the insecure dog can throw itself into a tizzy, howling, barking, or rushing about frantically, in dreaded anticipation of its owner's departure. The fear of being left alone can even cause these dogs to destroy furnishings or even lose their housetraining.

The crazed "return home" also works to generate undesirable canine behaviors, including jumping, excited urination, destructive behavior, or unwanted barking. High-energy dogs (especially puppies) could just lose it and run around like a jack rabbit the moment the owner starts gushing and cooing. Most distasteful.

As usual, these situations are usually caused by owners who don't quite understand what's going on in their dogs' heads. Let's look at each behavior separately.

A big mistake that a well-meaning owner can often make when coming home is to greet his or her dog in a manic, full-blown manner, with a big "I MISSED YOU, BOY!" followed by a crazy display of frenzied activity (such as running around the home, wrestling, or chasing). All this does is teach a dog that whenever someone comes through that front door, it's okay (and expected) to go nuts.

In place of such a spectacular greeting ritual, the owner should try coming into the home calmly—and even hold off on greeting the dog for a few minutes. Then, he or she should have the dog sit. After calmly praising it, the owner should move on and ignore the dog for a few minutes. Defusing the greeting ritual in this way will calm the excitable pooch, and teach it focus. Much better than a crazy "pinball" dog, right?

Separation anxiety can be a real bummer for some dogs, especially for strays and those rescued from a shelter. Some of these poor troopers panic at the thought of being left alone for even short periods. This behavior is often amplified by the owner making too big of a deal over the "departure" event. A melodramatic scene at the door can inevitably become a "dread initiator" for the pet. The mere thought of being abandoned can become a nightmare for the less than confident pet.

The classic, damaging departure ritual begins with

the owner kneeling down, lavishing the anxious dog with kisses, and saying something like: "Oh, Fifi, don't worry, honey, I'm only going to the store—I'll be right back; but I love you sooo much. . . ." Ugh. All this does is set the dog up, and announce that it's about to be left.

Instead, for ten minutes prior to leaving, your owner should *completely ignore you*. When she is ready to go, she should just *go*. No sad melodrama, no drawn out emotional pap. She can even use the back door, to really throw you off. By using these techniques, she'll help defuse the departure ritual, and reduce your anxiety.

By getting you used to the idea of her coming and going without fanfare or emotion, these techniques make such events become normal, ordinary, even forgetful to you. They certainly aren't experiences to become manic or anxious over, just simply part of the day. Remember, calm canine behavior most often occurs during the status quo. If you think all is normal, then the odds of undesirable behaviors occurring are reduced to a minimum.

Good luck, pal. Have her read this, and don't fret. Try blowing *her* off every now and then: It'll be a good lesson for her.

Handle Your Owner Every Day

Dear Gabby,

Last week I went home with a nice guy, after being in the shelter for two months. As I'm not exactly a spring chicken, I was grateful to find a place, and an owner willing to put up with me.

The problem is this guy wants to handle me all of the time. He tries to brush me, cut my nails (fat chance), and buddy up in a way that I'm not used to. Listen: When you spend time on the street, being touched usually means getting kicked or bitten. I'm just not too fond of all this new attention, if you know what I mean.

Gabby, how do I get this guy to lay off and let me be? I like him, but if he pets me while I'm sleeping again, I might bite him without meaning to. Help!

Sincerely,

Uptight in Umatilla

DEAR UPTIGHT,

I hear you, brother. I spent years on the street. When I finally found a good home, I didn't want anyone in the room when I ate, and I bit like a chain saw if somebody tried to brush me.

But here's the thing, pal: We are dogs. We're supposed to interact and enjoy physical contact. Unfortunately, abuse, homelessness, or trauma can cause some of us to fear contact. A shame, really, because once you learn to trust, it's really quite enjoyable.

Listen: He only means well, but is probably rushing things a bit. He needs to give you some space for a while, and let you ease into the new situation. You have to understand that he doesn't mean you harm, and that he needs contact as much as you do.

Owners who try too hard to create a bond with a rescue dog can often get into trouble, especially in the grooming department. Cut *whose* nails? Get outta town, dude! Instead, he should ease you into being touched, by linking it to things you *do* like, such as treats, dinner, or playtime.

Several factors could explain why a dog hates being handled. If you're a dog who has experienced physical abuse in the past, odds are you won't feel very comfortable being handled, even by a caring, gentle owner. A dog who has been teased by children may have similar feelings. Rescued pets or long-time strays tend to become aloof and uncomfortable when being handled, as they have had to struggle to survive, and may feel confined or endangered when handled.

A shy dog usually allows its owner to handle it, but may not be comfortable with guests trying to do the same. The dog reaches a point where it feels pressured, unsafe, or out of control, and must then put an end to the handling, even if it feels good.

Some dominant dogs abruptly decide that they have had enough handling, even though they might have been enjoying the attention right up to the moment of rejection. These dogs seem to genuinely enjoy being touched, but quickly reach a saturation point, whereupon they break off contact.

A dog separated from its litter before the eighth week of life may not have received the proper amount of socialization needed to become a well-rounded, confident adult. These dogs often shun the physical attentions of others. Though normally affectionate with its owner, this type of pet might object to being touched by guests.

So, what's the answer? An aversion to being handled or groomed usually stems from either fear or dominance issues, making a solution to the problem difficult.

The first step, as always, is to prevent problems before they arise. First, potential owners should only adopt or purchase a dog that has been allowed to stay with its mother and littermates until at least the eighth week. Doing so ensures that the pet has learned proper etiquette and socialization skills, by participating in mutual grooming sessions with the whole canine family. If that can't be ascertained before adoption or purchase, the dog or puppy in question should be handled and played with, to determine if it enjoys being touched.

Longhaired breeds dislike grooming more than their shorthaired kin because of the greater chance of tangles or matted hair. It takes longer to groom a longhaired dog, also, requiring them to tolerate the procedure for a longer period of time. The owner who chooses a shorthaired breed helps minimize the grooming issue, as short hair takes only a few moments to brush out.

Grooming sessions should begin early in a dog's life. Puppies should be handled as much as possible, and rewarded with occasional small treats during the procedure. An owner should begin by lightly running a comb or brush through the dog's hair once or twice each day—for just a minute or so—again, giving the dog treats during the session. By doing so, the dog will become accustomed to the procedure, and not resist it.

If your dog is showing a new dislike for grooming, it might have a sore spot or abscess on its skin. Owners should check for this: If something out of the ordinary is found, it's off to the veterinarian.

If an adult dog simply hates to be groomed but must

have it done, the owner should let a professional groomer do the job. He or she has plenty of experience in dealing with stressed or unruly dogs, and has the proper equipment and attitude to get the job done. If the dog's owner does it, odds are his or her dog will become upset, and possibly hold a grudge. By allowing a groomer to "take the heat," owners avoid damaging the relationship.

Trimming nails can be an especially risky venture for an inexperienced owner. To prevent a dog from disliking the procedure, owners should start early, and only clip the very tips of the nails, avoiding the little vein in the middle (called the "quick"). If an owner has any doubts or hesitation, a groomer should do the job.

A timid dog should never be forced to accept handling. When the unsure pet does seem open to being touched, it should be done gently and happily, as if the procedure is a happy game. The handling session should end while the dog still seems to be enjoying it, to assure that the entire experience will be enjoyed the next time. And as always, the owner also should reward with an occasional tasty treat during the handling session to reinforce and encourage the behavior.

The owner of a shy dog shouldn't expect the pet to accept handling from guests, particularly young children, who can be unpredictable and rough. Guests can offer the dog treats, however: They should place the tidbit on the floor near the pooch's feet, encouraging it to come close.

To help prevent a dog from becoming shy, the caring owner should handle it regularly from the first day. The dog should be treated gently, and be rewarded with a treat or two. Children should be taught to be gentle, and to not force a dog into being handled.

Above all, an owner should never strike his or her dog, as this will probably cool it to handling forever. Any corrections that need to be done should be administered with a leash and training collar. Also, the dog should be neutered (sorry), as doing so will remove the undesirable effects that hormonal peaks and valleys can have on mood and accessibility.

A dominant dog, or one with no obedience training, often objects to being groomed or handled, as it is a form of domination on the owner's part. These dogs can be a handful to groom or handle, and can readily show aggression when pushed. The best solution for these dogs is for the owner to get them both into an obedience class right away, to learn how to gain some control and leadership, and to take that pushy dog down a few notches in the hierarchy. But it sounds like you aren't this far gone, so maybe you'll have an easier time making the adjustment.

Uptight, I feel your pain. I was there. But at some point, you're going to need to let go and trust this guy. He sounds like he's trying, and has a good heart. Next time he tries to scratch you behind the ear, go with the moment. You just might enjoy it!

Overeaters Anonymous

Dear Gabby,

    I am an eight-year-old Boston terrier female who just can't get through the doggy door anymore. It's just not wide enough. Funny thing is, I never used to have a problem; this just started in the last six months or so. My owner got pretty upset with me yesterday for messing in the house, but what else could I do?

    Any advice, Gabby? I'm not very handy with tools, so I think a remodel is out.

    Your fan,

    Stuck in Stamford

DEAR STUCK,

You don't need a carpenter, you need a diet! Seriously, hon, the reason you can't get through that little door anymore is the expansion of your waistline. Like the rest of us middle-aged pets, time has a way of broadening our horizons, so to speak.

Odds are you've put on a few pounds, girlfriend. I'm not positive why, but I can take a few good guesses. Here are the reasons why a dog can gain weight:

- You are reaching middle age (six to eight years), and your metabolism may be slowing down. Your body burns fewer calories, but your appetite stays the same, and your owner feeds you the same amount each day. That leads to obesity.
- Your owner free-feeds you, instead of feeding you at specific times. Free-feeding means that food is kept in your dish all day, and you eat whenever you feel like it. When this is done, it's very hard for him or her to keep tabs on just how much you are eating. Your owner simply keeps topping off the dish when it gets low. You might be eating twice as much as you need. (This issue is covered in more depth in the next letter, so be sure to read it.)
- Your owner is giving you too many treats, or you're a beggar.

- ◆ You are stealing another pet's food.
- ◆ You are lazy.
- ◆ You have a metabolic problem.

Any one of these (or a combination of two or more) could be causing you to put on the pounds. Do any of them sound familiar? Here is what you need to do, hon, in order to get yourself through the doggy door again:

- ◆ Get your owner to take you to the vet, to rule out any medical problems that might be contributing to your weight gain. An underactive thyroid gland would cause a dog to gain weight, so get that checked.
- ◆ If you are being free-fed, have your owner begin feeding you on a precise schedule to keep track of the food you eat. Your vet should be able to advise your owner on how much food is just right.
- ◆ Stop begging at the dinner table!
- ◆ Your owner needs to stop spoiling you with treats all day. If you get treats, the food you get at dinner time should be reduced accordingly.
- ◆ Are you eating another pet's food? If so, have your owner feed that pet in another room, away from you.
- ◆ You need more exercise. Get your owner

to take you for a long walk each day, or get to the dog park, where you can run with other pooches and burn calories.

◆ Have your owner switch you over to a lower-calorie "senior" food. This will allow you to eat the same volume of food, but take in fewer calories.

◆ Have your owner cut your food by 10 percent, and replace the lost amount with well-cooked green beans, which are very low in calories.

Abiding by any or all of these techniques should help you get back that girlish figure, Stuck. Good luck, and suck in that gut!

Free-Feeding?
Forget About It!

Dear Gabby,

Something strange has been happening to my appetite. I'm a big, mixed-breed male carrying a few extra pounds, but you wouldn't know it to see me eat. Food just doesn't seem to move me like it used to. I remember how hearing the sound of the scoop into the food bag would give me goose bumps and send me running for my bowl. Now, I couldn't care less. The best I can do is nibble a little bit throughout the day. It's not like the food isn't available; my owner even recently started leaving food out for me while he's gone. It doesn't taste all that bad, either; it just doesn't pull my tail like it used to.

Gabby, is there something wrong with me? You don't think I have any kind of disease, do you? Help me out, if you can.

Respectfully,

Blasé in Santa Fe

DEAR BLASÉ,

No need to sweat it, kid. You're not sick or crazy, you've just desensitized. Let me explain.

Because so many owners spend hours away from home during the day, they often come to the conclusion that their dogs must either be starving, or bored to tears. While the latter might be true, the former certainly isn't. Nevertheless, they make the decision to leave food down for their pets, a technique called *free-feeding*. I discussed it briefly in the last letter, "Overeaters Anonymous," but here I'll need to go into a bit more detail.

Free-feeding is practiced by owners who think it will in some way occupy the pets' time or be a comfort. Some owners use this method even while home, and simply replenish the supply whenever it's diminished.

This practice can cause a number of problems, obesity being the primary one. When a dog has a constant supply of food available, it will quickly reach a state in which it is not ever really hungry, but instead always nearly satiated. This pet will end up picking at its food all day. Though eating less at each feeding, the pet ends up cumulatively eating more than if the owner had fed it one or two distinct twenty-minute meals per day.

The lesson learned here is that all-day "snacking" leads not only to obesity, but to a severely reduced food drive in the affected animal. If food is always there, why should you ever get excited over it?

Another negative aspect of free-feeding us dogs is that it causes our digestive processes to go on nearly nonstop throughout the day. This causes us to become sleepy and lethargic, discouraging any kind of calorie-burning activity from taking place. Any pet who is constantly lying around digesting has a slower metabolism, resulting in lower caloric expenditures.

The practice of free-feeding does not benefit even a finicky, underweight pet. In thinking that supplying a constant source of food will encourage a thin dog to put on weight, owners of these pets actually accomplish the opposite. Think about it: What conditions must occur in the wild for a wolf or tiger to become famished? Certainly not one of abundance. Why be ravenous with a constantly full belly? Consequently, their prey (or food) drive diminishes.

Animal trainers who work with large predators know that if you want to reduce the chances of an attack, simply make sure that the animal is well fed. Providing a finicky pet with a constant supply of food actually lowers its food drive, further compounding the problem. So, free-feeding fattens up pets with normal or high food drives, and makes finicky eaters even more selective.

Make sense, Blasé? Here's what needs to happen. Somehow you must convince your owner to feed you two meals per day, at exact times. One in the early morning, and another in the evening works for me. He should leave the food down for a maximum of fifteen minutes, then pick up whatever is left and save it for the next feeding time. By doing so, he will help reestablish a food drive in you. You'll start looking forward to dinnertime again, and should even lose a few pounds in the process. Your energy levels will shoot up as well.

As far as boredom during the day, have him read my letter called "Bored Brainless!" That'll give him numerous ways to keep you occupied during the day.

Don't worry! There's nothing wrong with you that a well-anticipated meal can't cure. Bon Appétit!

Subpar Food

Dear Gabby,

My owner's taste in dog food has suddenly become pretty shoddy, if you ask me. Up until last week, she was feeding me a tasty dry food that we always bought at the pet shop each month. Then, for some strange reason, she started feeding me this strange-smelling supermarket swill. It tastes like cardboard, and doesn't even look very appetizing. I miss the old food something awful, Gabby, and have already lost weight (not a good idea for a whippet). Any ideas?

Your friend,

Scrawny in Schenectady

DEAR SCRAWNY,

Sounds like a little belt-tightening might be going on here, pal. Sorry about the change in menu; might be your owner's taste in dog food has taken a nose dive. First, let's talk a bit about dog food, and what's needed to keep a dog healthy and happy.

There are five basic types of food available for you to eat today. These include the following:

- Pet-store dry food
- Supermarket dry food
- Canned food
- Semimoist food
- Home-cooked food

Pet-Store Dry Food

Pet-store dry pet foods normally have a high degree of quality, both in the ingredients and in the processes used to create the product. Manufactured in smaller batches and sold at higher prices, these foods are normally made with good ingredients, including fresh meat and grains, few if any preservatives, and a complete spectrum of the necessary vitamins and minerals. The formula of the food itself is often more carefully thought out and monitored with pet-store dry foods than with supermarket brands; percentages of protein, fat, carbohydrates, and other ingredients are carefully adjusted to match the unique needs of the pet, regardless of age. Overall, I recommend pet-store dry foods, if your owner doesn't mind paying $30 to $35 dollars for a forty-pound bag.

Supermarket Dry Food

Supermarket dry foods, sold by the millions of bags each year, tend to be less expensive than what is available in pet shops. These foods usually contain higher levels of preservatives, coloring agents, and taste enhancers, and can also have measurable levels of pesticide residue and residual amounts of antibiotics and hormones used in the raising of the meat that goes into the mixture. Cheaper brands may contain low-quality meat and meat by-products not approved for human consumption by the USDA (United States Department of Agriculture). The term "meat by-products" can legally include beaks, feathers, bones, heads, organs, skin, and even fecal material (yuck!). It is even perfectly legal for dog and cat food companies to use diseased or dying animals in their foods.

Most of the big name supermarket dry foods, however, now produce a quality product that will promote good health. If your owner has chosen this option, you can feel safe that you're getting adequate nutrition at a reasonable price. Be sure that the food your owner chooses uses real meat instead of meat by-products.

Whether your owner chooses a supermarket or pet-shop food, make sure it has these things:

- the proper nutrient balance for your age
- a freshness date somewhere on the package, as well as the manufacturer's guarantee that the product is nutritionally complete
- meat as the first ingredient listed on the label
- whole, cooked grains instead of grain "fractions," such as peanut hulls, empty grain husks, or even sawdust
- As few artificial ingredients and preservatives as possible

Canned Food

Canned pet food can provide adequate nutrition for a dog, and as an added bonus has a very long shelf life. Available in a wide variety of quality levels, this type of food can be fed alone, or as a supplement to dry food. Canned pet food can be primarily meat based, or have a cereal content high enough to require it to be listed as the primary ingredient. For us, the food we eat should have meat as its main ingredient, so be sure your owner avoids canned foods made primarily of grain.

Canned food contains 50 to 70 percent water. This has its good and bad sides.

The good side is that it resembles food found in the wild, and as such will supply the dog or cat with more moisture than dry food. This can, over time, help prevent kidney disease caused by a chronic lack of water in the pet's diet. The extra water also can make elimination easier.

On the bad side, the high water content makes canned food much more expensive and less nutritious on a pound-for-pound basis. Your owner ends up paying for water instead of food.

As in dry pet foods, the quality of canned food varies considerably, price often being the tip off. Cheap supermarket canned foods have the same drawbacks as cheap dry foods: poor meat sources and a high percentage of poor-quality grains, preservatives, and other undesirable ingredients. Pet shops carry higher-quality brands of canned food, at a higher price. As a rule, your owner should avoid canned food that costs less than a dollar per twelve-ounce can.

Semimoist Food

This type of pet food is often used as an alternative to canned or dry. Lighter and easier to store, these semimoist, burger-type foods are very palatable to most dogs. They are on the expensive side, however, and often contain high amounts of preservatives, artificial colorings, binders, and sugar—ingredients needed to give the food its meatlike texture. Though capable of providing adequate nutrition, semimoist food is probably the least desirable of the commercially available foods. If it were up to me, I'd avoid them.

Home-Cooked Food

More and more owners are preparing their pets' foods right in their own kitchens. Using fresh, raw or lightly cooked meats, cooked whole grains, cooked vegetables, and various other ingredients, many caring owners with time on their hands prepare meals for us that are not only good-tasting, but superior to commercial foods in several ways. In addition to being fresh, home-cooked pet food is free of artificial ingredients and potentially harmful chemicals such as pesticides, hormones, antibiotics, and preservatives. The meat used is generally only lightly cooked or raw, assuring that it contains the highest possible amounts of necessary nutrients.

Commercial foods are often subjected to high cooking temperatures for long periods of time, rendering their nutrients less beneficial. The meat used in home-cooked pet food needn't be cooked, provided it is fresh, as our digestive tracts are designed to efficiently deal with raw meat, due to stronger digestive acids and enzymes.

Whatever supermarket food your owner has switched you to, she needs to first make sure that it contains all the necessary nutrients, with as few preservatives as possible. If it does, the next problem is taste. Obviously, you aren't thrilled with it. She probably switched you over too quickly. Doing that, in addition to sometimes causing diarrhea, can be too much of a shock on a dog's taste buds. She should have switched you over more slowly, over a 2- to 3-week period of time. She can gradually blend in more of the new food and less of the old. That way, the taste issue wouldn't be so noticeable to you.

If she needs to save money and keep you on a supermarket food, a good way for her to get you to like it is for her to buy a few cans of high-quality pet store canned food. Then she can mix 2 or 3 tablespoons of it into the new food, along with some warm water. If she lets it soak in for a few minutes, you might start liking the taste. Or, she can mix in some chicken or beef broth, or even toss in a few tablespoons of finely chopped bits of real meat. This should pep up the taste, while only minimally affecting cost.

Good luck, Scrawny; have her read this letter, and maybe things will get a little tastier for you.

Exercising Essentials

Dear Gabby,

As a two-year-old boxer mix, let me tell you, I love my exercise. Used to be every day my owner would take me down to the park in the morning; we'd play ball for a while, then go down to the dog area, where my buddies and I would catch up on all the news.

Then the unthinkable happened. She got a nine-to-five job, with an hour commute each way. Not only did I have to kiss our morning jaunts good-bye, but now she's so tired at night that the best I get is a quick frolic in the backyard.

Gabby, I'm putting on the pounds, and going stir-crazy. An athlete like me needs to run and jump and swim and cavort every day. Without it, I think I'll lose my marbles. Any advice?

Your pal,
Edgy in Arcadia

DEAR EDGY,

You boxers are so buff. An athlete like you must be going bonkers without an outlet for all that energy. Let me try to help.

The typical domestic dog lives a rather mundane, sluggish life. Most healthy dogs would rather be participating in some form of energetic activity during the day, but, given no other option, they sit around twiddling their paws. This can lead not only to weight gain, but to serious stress and behavioral problems.

The problem is caused by owners who often do not have the time to exercise their pets, or who simply think that their furry friends just don't need it, that they are pets, with naturally high metabolisms. Wrong! Dogs today, especially those kept in urban settings, often get less exercise than their owners, who, in addition to working 8 to 10 hours per day, work out at gyms, jog, cycle, or play sports when time allows. When was the last time you had that active a day?

Exercise, for pets and humans alike, is a vital ingredient to physical and mental well-being. In addition to burning calories, it raises the metabolic "thermostat" of the body, allowing you to burn more calories at rest than would otherwise be possible. Exercise builds muscle as well; as muscles are calorie "engines," having them more developed helps burn more calories.

In addition, exercise has a profoundly positive effect on

mood and attitude. During strenuous activity, the endocrine systems of dogs, like humans, produce endorphins, naturally occurring hormones that help create a positive, alert, almost euphoric mindset. Those pets who exercise on a regular basis become more confident, happy, and psychologically sound than those who never lift a finger. Therapists who work with people suffering from depression always prescribe exercise to their patients for this reason.

It stands to reason, then, that exercise should become a mandatory component of every dog's day. Without it, you will become overweight and depressed, and could become a behavioral problem.

The problem for you is made worse by your breed, I'm sorry to say. Boxers are high-energy dogs, and must be allowed to exercise at least once per day. I'm surprised you haven't had a nervous breakdown yet.

Here's what your owner needs to do, Edgy. First, she needs to take you for a walk in the early morning, before she leaves for work. Even a 10-minute trip around the block will do. It'll mean getting up 10 minutes earlier, but that's not too unreasonable, if she expects to own a boxer.

Next, she needs to get a neighbor or a pet walker to come over during the day, to take you for

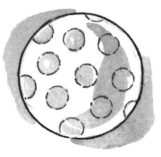

a walk, or to the park. Two or three times per week would be the minimum; once per day is ideal. If she can't do this for you, then she shouldn't own a boxer. You're not a Persian cat, for goodness sake.

When she gets home, have her take you into the yard for a quick game of fetch before dinner. Five minutes should do. Then, on weekends, she should take you to the dog park once or twice, so you can run around with your cronies. If a swim could be tossed into the mix, all the better.

Lastly, be sure she monitors your food intake, and adjusts it accordingly. We don't want that athletic body of yours to go to pot, right?

Good luck, pal. Get her on board for these changes, and you should start feeling better soon.

When Your Owner Is a Wimp

Dear Gabby,

For many years I had it good. Slept in the owner's bed, ate from the table, begged my way into obesity, and generally ruled the roost. The old guy was a wimp, but I didn't care, because I called the shots.

Then he had to go into a nursing home. It was pretty upsetting, as we'd been together for ten years. I'm living with his son's family now, and it's hell. They don't let me up on the furniture or beds, and I'm not allowed to eat off of the table. I can't growl at strangers coming into the home, or at the kids, who seem to think they are more important than me.

Yesterday I bit the wife when she tried to cut my nails. Hey, let me tell you, nobody cuts *my* nails. Anyway, I've been in a dog crate now for 6 hours (can you imagine?), and don't know what will happen next. Can you help me, Gabby?

Your fellow canine,
Misunderstood in Missoula

DEAR MISUNDERSTOOD,

Sorry, pal, but you're barking up the wrong tree. Sounds like you ruled the roost at your last pad, and were quite content doing so. Well, I'm one dog who thinks that we canines should not take on the burden of the "Alpha" role, as it's a big responsibility, and can get us into all sorts of trouble, as you are finding out now.

When you lived with your first owner, he let you take on the position of leader. You ate whatever you wanted, slept in the best spots, decided on who was and who wasn't welcome in the home, and a litany of other "bossy" behaviors. Paradise, I guess, if you like that kind of power trip. By allowing you to take over, your owner wimped out on his responsibilities as the leader of his pack. You became the boss, and quickly began to set up your own little kingdom.

Now the tide has turned. You think you still have the right to rule, but that power is gone, pal. Where in the past you might have gotten away with biting or growling, now that just won't work. This new family will not put up with a dog being the head honcho, and if you can't get that through your thick skull, odds are you'll end up in a shelter, with nowhere else to go. Consider yourself lucky, and try to get with the program.

Your former owner goofed, pal. He should have established himself as the "Alpha" dog in the pack, but didn't. But it was okay, because he was the only one you came in contact with. Mistakes he probably made include the following:

- Allowing you to sleep in bed with him
- Allowing you to make the leash tight during walks
- Feeding you first
- Letting you rush through doors before him
- Allowing you up on the furniture
- Allowing you to dominate him with body positioning
- Allowing you to greet friends and strangers before him
- Acquiescing to your every demand
- Playing chase games and tug-of-war
- Roughhousing

Any or all of these errors in ownership can create a dominant, pushy pooch, one who will sooner or later suffer because of increasingly dangerous behaviors. How long do you think you can get away with biting people, tough guy?

Your new owners, if they choose to keep you, need to regain leadership, and get you to see the light. This may not be possible without professional help, but at least they can follow some basic guidelines to take you down a notch or two. These include:

- Feeding you last
- Keeping you off of furniture and beds

- Seeing to it that you earn every treat, privilege, or pet on the head
- Not allowing you to greet strangers first
- Not roughhousing or playing tug-of-war with you
- Never allowing you to take a dominant posture, such as lying atop someone
- Not allowing you to pull while on the leash
- Not ever letting you growl at a member of the family without punishment

If they follow these guidelines and get a professional canine behaviorist to help, maybe, just maybe, they'll save your pushy butt from the clink. Good luck, Misunderstood; you're going to need it!

Love That Vet!

Dear Gabby,

Well, I've gone and done it again. While running around the yard, I stepped in a hole and tweaked my shoulder pretty bad. Thing is, I'm eight years old now, and a pretty big boy, with achy joints. Hurting my shoulder like this just compounds the problem.

I've been hiding the pain, because, well, I despise going to the veterinarian. It's not that she's all that bad a person; it's just that whenever I'm there, bad things happen. Whether it's a nail clipping, shots, or a temperature check, I just hate everything in the place. She squeezes me, sticks stuff down my throat, and makes my achy joints hurt more by moving them all over the place. And who could like those slippery tables? And the lighting? Ugh!

Sooner or later my owner is going to catch the limp, Gabby. Is there any way you can think of for me to avoid the vet? Maybe yoga, or acupuncture? I'll try anything!

Eternally yours,

Frightened in Fremont

DEAR FRIGHTENED,

I hear you, pal. I once had to get a dirty sock cut out of my intestines. What can I say? I was young. Anyway, that veterinarian didn't exactly have the best bedside manners. He got the sock out, though.

Most dogs do not savor going to the veterinarian—even for annual checkups. After all, being poked and prodded by a total stranger isn't anyone's idea of a fun afternoon. Your temperature is taken (not pleasant), blood may be drawn, and your ears and mouth must be examined. During all of this, many a pet simply can't sit still, which sometimes means the veterinarian and his or her assistants have to "immobilize" it just to finish the exam. As this may be the only contact you and the veterinarian ever experience, you can understand why the mere sight of the clinic might depress you.

Some fearful dogs resist the probing and restraining, and try to extricate themselves from the situation, often by growling, or biting. Some give in quickly, while others fight to the end, requiring a muzzle and some strong hands. Most dogs fall somewhere in between, making sure veterinarians earn their pay.

From your point of view, the veterinarian is a controlling bully. You do not feel at all comfortable with a total stranger taking such physical liberties. When the veterinarian persists, you can begin to fear the situation. With nowhere to run, though, you may panic and try to fight your way to freedom, which usually fails, and creates great, lasting trauma.

Dogs have good memories. If someone accidentally (or otherwise) hurts a dog, it might retain that memory forever, and may never feel at ease around that person again. Such is the lot of the veterinarian. In trying to examine and treat the dog, he or she can create a humiliating and scary situation for the pet, who will forever retain the memory and resist the veterinarian's wishes, no matter how careful and gentle he or she is.

Owners can help make the veterinarian's life a bit easier. One way to do it is for them to handle their dogs each and every day, starting early on. From the very first day an owner should regularly pick up his dog, examine its body, look into its ears and mouth, and check its coat and skin for parasites. He should brush and comb it frequently, and give it a delicious treat as a reward after each handling or grooming session. It's too late for you to be a puppy again, Frightened, but by desensitizing you to examination from a very early age, your owner would have been making your veterinarian's job much easier. Doing so would ultimately help keep you in the best shape possible.

Since you're a dog who already hates going to the veterinarian, there isn't much

that can be done, except to attempt to alter your opinion of the place. You and your owner should try visiting the veterinarian's office every now and then for a "nonvisit." He should take you in for a quick "hello" from the staff there, who can (if time allows) pet you and give you treats. You and your owner can even play with each other right there in the office, provided there are no other animals in the reception area. Take along your favorite ball and have a go at it for a minute. Live it up for a bit, then leave. If the staff at the clinic is tolerant of your doing this, it will help to at least partially diffuse your fears of going there.

A few pets become so fear-aggressive that they must be sedated in order to be examined. If this is the case with you, your owner should ask your veterinarian to prescribe a mild sedative that can be given to you before the visit. Normally provided in pill form, the sedative will calm you down enough to allow the exam to take place.

Don't fear the vet, pal; next to your owner, she might be the most important human in your life. With a little help from your owner, the trip there shouldn't be much worse than getting a bath.

Looking Good, Baby!

Dear Gabby,

I'm a three-year-old Afghan female who hates to be groomed. I spend a good deal of time out in the yard, and my long coat gets pretty snarled and dirty. Even though the mats I get can become a real nuisance, I fight off any of my owner's attempts to comb them out. It hurts!

Gabby, I have a feeling that I'll be heading for the groomer soon. Last time that happened, I had to be muzzled and sedated. Still, she had to attach all sorts of leashes and straps to me to keep me in place. To add insult to injury, she cut my nails, something I never let my owner do.

Here's my question: Is there any way for me to get out of this? Can I groom myself during the day when my owner is gone? Help, Gabby!

Affectionately,

Matted in Madison

DEAR MATTED,

You Afghans are sooo good-looking! Can't imagine your long, lustrous locks all snarled and tangled, though. You must be one of those earthy Afghans. Anyway, it's a shame, because there's nothing so nice as a beautifully maintained, silky coat.

Some dogs develop a dislike for being groomed, and either run away from or nip the person attempting to do it. The dog in question may see the comb or brush and head for the hills, or else assume a submissive, defensive posture, with its ears laid back and its tail between its legs. The dog may struggle, growl, or even physically injure the groomer.

Several reasons might explain this behavior. The pet might have had a bad experience at one time, with the groomer accidentally catching the comb or brush in a matted section of coat, resulting in a painful pull on the skin. Or, the dog might have had a groomer improperly restrain it in order to complete the procedure. Just one upsetting grooming event can sour a dog on the procedure forever.

A dog who has had its nails clipped too short while being groomed feels a good deal of pain, due to the "quick" (a blood vessel and nerve bundle running inside the nail) being cut. The quick grows fairly close to the nail tip; inexperienced owners often cut it accidentally, causing much bleeding and discomfort. Any dog who has had this occur fears the procedure.

There are other reasons why a dog like you would hate to be groomed. If you were abused physically in the past, you probably wouldn't feel comfortable with all the brushing and combing; you just never learned that being touched could be fun. Dogs who have been around children who tease them a lot have the same reaction: Touching can seem like torture.

You probably aren't a rescued dog, but they (along with long-time strays) generally dislike the whole grooming thing. They usually look totally uncomfortable, like they can barely stand it. That's because, after spending so much time roaming free on the streets and trying to survive, they distrust anything that seems confining. It feels downright dangerous to be under someone's complete control, and plain inconvenient to stand still so long.

A shy dog usually allows its owner to handle it, but may not be comfortable with guests trying to do the same. The dog reaches a point where it feels pressured, unsafe, or out of control, and must then put an end to the handling, even if it feels good.

Longhaired breeds like you dislike grooming more than their shorthaired kin, because of the greater chance of tangles or matted hair. It takes longer to groom a longhaired dog, also, requiring you guys—and gals—to tolerate the procedure for a longer period of time. Tough being a diva, huh?

Owners should begin grooming sessions early in their dog's life. Puppies should be handled and brushed as much as possible, and rewarded with occasional small treats during the procedure. A gentle, light combing once or twice each day, combined with a tasty treat each time, does wonders for a dog's tolerance. That's how my first owner got me to like being groomed, and I've craved it ever since.

Some dogs develop a sudden dislike for grooming due to a new sore spot or abscess on their skin. Get your owner to check for these regularly; if something is found, see your veterinarian.

If you simply hate to be groomed but must have it done, your owner should let a professional groomer do the job. He or she has plenty of experience in dealing with stressed or unruly dogs, and will have the proper equipment and attitude to get the job done properly. If your owner attempts it, odds are you will become upset, and possibly show aggression. By allowing a groomer to "take the heat," your owner can avoid damaging his or her relationship with you. Trimming nails can be an especially risky venture for an inexperienced owner; if yours has any doubts about his or her ability to do so, a pro should do it instead.

A timid dog should be groomed gently and positively, with care taken around touchy areas such as the rump, groin, or neck. The owner should always end the grooming session while the dog still seems to be enjoying it, as well, to assure that the entire experience remains an enjoyable one. Your owner should always reward you with an occasional tasty treat during the session, also, to reinforce and encourage the behavior.

An owner should never physically punish his or her dog for fearing the grooming session, as this will probably cool it to handling forever. Any corrections that need to be done to address aggression should be administered with a leash and training collar.

The owner of a pushy, dominant dog should consider having the dog neutered (if it hasn't already been done). Doing that removes the undesirable effects that hormonal peaks and valleys can have on mood and accessibility. Dominant dogs may abruptly decide that they have had enough grooming, even though they might have been enjoying the attention right up to the moment of rejection. These dogs seem to genuinely enjoy being touched, but quickly reach a saturation point, whereupon they must break off the contact.

A dominant dog (or one with no obedience training) will often object to being groomed or handled, as it is a form of domination on the owner's part. These dogs can be a handful to groom or handle, and can readily show aggression when pushed. Are you one of these?

The solution for these dogs is twofold: First, your owner should get the both of you into an obedience class right away, to allow him or her to gain some control and leadership, and to take you down a few notches in the hierarchy. Second, if the dominant dog needs grooming, again, its owner should let a professional groomer do it, without the owner present. Groomers make a living dealing with uncooperative dogs, and won't have much of a problem.

Matted, you need to chill out and let someone comb and brush out those nasty mats and snarls. If you don't, you'll become dirtier and more uncomfortable as the weeks go by. I have a feeling that a combination of touch desensitization by your owner and a session with a top-notch groomer will solve your problem. Let your owner stroke and lightly brush you each day, in exchange for a treat or two. He or she doesn't even have to detangle you, but merely go through the motions. By doing so, you will learn not to fear the procedure so much. Then, it's off to the groomer!

The Stressed-out Owner

Dear Gabby,

I'm a two-year-old Doberman male recently adopted by a middle-aged woman. We live in the country, and have few visitors. I think she got me less for companionship and more for protection, as she seems scared and nervous all the time. When the telephone rings, she jumps. If a storm comes up, she crawls under the bed covers and trembles. It's not exactly confidence inspiring, let me tell you.

To top it off, she argues with her neighbor all the time, over weird things, like how tall a tree is, or if the hedge needs trimming. Who cares? Anyway, they yell at each other a lot, causing me to bark and hide under the bed.

Gabby, I'm beginning to get stressed-out by her stress. I'd like to just be a dog, but I feel as if I have to be protector, master, and psychiatrist, all rolled into one. It's nerve-wracking, and not what I expected. Any advice?

Your loyal fan,

Strained in Sturgis

DEAR STRAINED,

Why don't you just take her to that big old biker rally? That'd chill her out. She seriously sounds like a nervous Nellie. Owners like her often get dogs for protection, but fail to realize that dogs, being very attuned to an owner's moods, mirror the atmosphere of the home. If she projects insecurity and stress, odds are you will begin to as well. When the pack leader isn't confidence inspiring, the pack members become worrisome and insecure. This can lead to behavioral problems such as the following:

◆ Housetraining mishaps
◆ Fear aggression
◆ Destructive behavior
◆ Barking

Your owner isn't being a very good leader. She sounds like a shrinking violet, and doesn't seem to have much happiness in her life. What a bummer.

Problem is, her downbeat, nervous attitude is going to rub off on you and make you cuckoo. If she really cared, she would take your well-being into consideration, and clean up her act. Here's what she should do. If you can, get her to read this, okay?

First, she should interact with you in a happier, confident manner, as often as possible. Have her throw a ball around for you, or teach you a few tricks. Second, get her to have more people over to the house. The extra socialization will help both of you ease up and enjoy life a little more. She should also try to get you away from the home every now and then, maybe to a dog park, or for a walk downtown, where there is lots for you to see and smell.

By trying these things, your owner will help reduce the stress in the home for the both of you. Good luck, partner. Hey, maybe she can buy a chopper and join in Sturgis's summer festivities!

Replaced and Disgraced

Dear Gabby,

I think the honeymoon is over. For years I was top dog in the home; my owners catered to me like I was the crown prince. Nothing was too good for me, a five-year-old Saluki male in my prime. Home-cooked meals, walks in the park, gentle grooming, sleeping in their bed--I had it made. To them, I was their light, their hope, their motivation for living. Until last week, that is.

Enter the germ bag, the fire alarm, the stench bucket. Yeah, you guessed it: They had a baby. And it's here, *in this house.* It cries and poops and wets and lolls its eyes. That's it. Oh, and it nurses, and goes "goo goo" and "blah" every now and then. It can't run or jump or bark or beg or shake, and it can't fetch. And it sure as heck isn't going to win "best in show," let me tell you. Heck, the thing isn't even housetrained.

Nevertheless, it has basically taken over the home. Everyone fawns over it. Neighbors gawk at it and bring it presents. And my owners? They can't leave the darn thing alone for

more than a few minutes at a time--especially
since I got fed up and growled at it the
other day.

Me? I don't exist anymore. I'm lucky to be
let out or fed. Yesterday I didn't even get
breakfast. Once the apex of their existence, I
am now doo-doo.

Gabby, I loathe the little flesh ball.
He's taken everything away from me. I'm scared
that they might get rid of me, because of my
dirty looks and growling. What should I do?

Your slighted supporter,

Snubbed in San Diego

DEAR SNUBBED,

Easy, big fella. Don't get your lustrous locks all in a tangle. We can work this out, so lie down, breathe, then read.

When childless owners get a dog, they put much of their energies, emotions, and parental instincts into caring for it, and in making it feel like part of the family. As happened to you, the pet often becomes the focal point of their lives, the sole outlet for their love and attention.

When a new baby comes into the picture, though, the proud parents understandably shift their attentions from the dog to the newborn. Instinctively protective of their new, delicate little person, they might worry that the dog's nails, teeth, or lively personality might accidentally cause harm to the baby. Once the star of the show, the dog now becomes suspect when the child is present.

Unfortunately, new parents often forget that their dog is still part of the family, and has needs too. With all of the attention going to the new baby, you are feeling alienated and left out, as if you were no longer part of the "pack." While the baby gets all of the attention, you get chastised just for being near it. Poor dog, you've been effectively demoted from "top dog" to second-class citizen. Now resentment has resulted, leading to possible canine behavior problems, including disobedience, housetraining setbacks, destructive behavior, or even aggression toward the child or owner(s).

If an owner ignores a dog or yells at it when it's close to

the baby, that pet is going to start disliking the little tyke. That's just the way we dogs are wired. It's called a *conditioned response*. If you get a sore leg whenever it rains, you will start worrying the moment a cloud appears in the sky. Makes sense, right?

Most owners with newborn children have no clue that they're making their dogs feel unimportant. They just don't understand how crucial it is for canines to maintain their perceived status in the pack. When the appearance of a child causes estrangement, it's only natural for them to start thinking that the baby is the source of all their problems.

So, what to do? First, you need to lighten up, and stop growling at the kid. That's the quickest route to the shelter, pal, so lay off. Next, it sounds as if you might have had it too cushy before the baby came into the picture; sleeping in your owners' bed sounds a bit privileged to me. Can you say "spoiled"? If they hadn't made you the focus of all their attentions in the first place, you might not be having as hard a time of it now.

That said, your owners are ignoring your needs, and that's not good. Understandable given the circumstances, but not wise. The following are a number of ways they can help to

change the situation, and avoid any future problems between you and the child:

- Understand that the new baby must become a *positive influence* in your life. Whenever you are near the baby, they should *praise* you, and make you feel 10 feet tall. By doing so, they begin to teach you that the baby's presence equates to positive attention.
- They should give you one of the baby's blankets to sleep with, as soon as possible, to acclimate you to the child's smell.
- They should work your basic obedience skills (sit, down, stay) while around the child, and be sure to reward you with a treat or two when you perform well. That way you begin to understand that proper behavior around the baby gets you noticed, and praised.
- Anytime you show positive behavior toward the baby, they should praise you lavishly!
- They need to ensure that, in the future, the child never pulls on your ears or tail, or hurts you in any way. To the contrary, when the child is old enough, it should learn to gently pet you and give you praise and treats.

If your owners do these things on a regular basis, in no time you will actually begin enjoying the baby, instead of dreading it. Think of it: Whenever the newbie is near you,

you get hugs and cookies! Who wouldn't love a kid like that? Within no time, that baby will become your best buddy.

One note of caution: Your owners should never, ever leave you alone with the baby. Even a child-loving dog could accidentally hurt an infant, so they need to keep the door to the baby's room securely shut when you are in the home, and they are not there to supervise.

There is no excuse for them neglecting you, pal, despite the uniqueness of the event. Even though the baby needs lots of attention, you still need to be fed, stroked, loved, and taken for walks. You are part of the family too; in order for you to accept and love the baby, your owners must convince you that the child's presence brings happiness, not alienation. Now, grab your ball and drop it beside the baby; your owners will think it a cute gesture, and forget all about the growling. Pass this letter on to the proud parents, and watch things get better!

Severe Situations: When They Need Professional Help

Dear Gabby,

Things aren't much fun here anymore. A month ago, my owners adopted me, a male pit bull mix, and brought me home to a great place with a big backyard. Problem is, I don't much like other dogs, and their other pooch is a big shepherd mix who has it in for me. We fight every day while our owners are at work. Yesterday I hurt him pretty badly, after he bit the tip of my ear off. They had to take him in to the vet, where he got 40 stitches and a bunch of shots.

Gabby, I know when they bring him home, he's going to lay into me like the marines at Iwo Jima. Any advice? Should I run away, or stage a preemptive strike? Help!

Your friend,

Fighting in Fredericksburg

DEAR FIGHTING,

Sorry to hear about the bad times, dude. Sounds like it's been pretty rough in that backyard, and that it's only going to get rougher.

My feeling is that both you and your yard mate may have come from less than desirable neighborhoods and backgrounds. Being a rescue dog myself, I know how rough things can get. When a dog has to struggle to survive, sometimes aggression seems the only way to do it. Get him before he gets me, right?

Here's the scoop, pal. I don't know exactly why the two of you aren't getting along, and it's a sure bet that your owners don't either. But if things keep going the way they have been, one of you might soon end up on the short end of the leash. Normally two dogs work out their relationship in the pack pretty quickly, then take it from there. You two have deeper-seated issues of aggression going on, though, and it doesn't sound as if they will work themselves out anytime soon.

Sometimes owners need to bite the biscuit and call in professional help in order to solve a nasty canine behavioral problem. This is one of those times, pal. If they themselves try to mediate or eliminate the aggression problem between you two bruisers, they could make matters worse, or even end up getting hurt themselves. If that happens, one or both of you could end up sleeping for a long, long time.

Take my advice and have them call a professional canine

behaviorist. They can get a recommendation from your veterinarian. Trained to understand the canine psyche, this person is able to determine if the problem can be easily solved, or if it has its basis in some hereditary flaw that cannot be mediated. Without this expert help, I'm afraid the both of you are in for a sad, short run.

In addition to serious displays of aggression, there are other behavioral situations that can occur with us dogs that often cannot be handled by owners alone, and so require professional help. These include the following:

- ◆ Serious medical problems
- ◆ Chronic escaping
- ◆ Heavy-duty grooming needs
- ◆ The needs of a geriatric dog
- ◆ Profound behavioral problems
- ◆ Chronic housetraining woes
- ◆ The overanxious or worrisome dog

Any one of these situations can easily overwhelm the average owner's ability to cope. For instance, the owner of a long-haired dog with terrible tangles and mats in its coat won't be able to easily deal with the mess without possibly damaging the owner/dog relationship. Better to seek out

a professional groomer, who knows exactly how to approach the problem, and can do so with a minimum of fuss and anxiety.

The dog who constantly escapes and runs away is another example of a severe situation calling for professional help. Without being shown the correct way to teach the dog not to do this, its owners risk the unthinkable. Better for them to hire a good dog trainer to show them how to recondition the dog into not taking off.

The owner of a dog with serious health issues such as diabetes or chronic hip dysplasia can't deal with the situation without professional help, either. That's why calling in a qualified veterinarian is an essential move, one that could easily save a life.

Whatever the situation, if an owner can't seem to remedy it quickly, without injury or trauma, a professional should be called in to help. Canine professionals include:

- ◆ Canine behaviorists
- ◆ Obedience trainers
- ◆ Groomers
- ◆ Veterinarians
- ◆ Dog-sitters or daycares
- ◆ Boarding kennels

If the owner of a dog finds him- or herself in a situation too dangerous or traumatic to deal with, it's time to call in a pro, who knows what to do. In your case, you'll need to work with a canine behaviorist as soon as possible. Good luck, and peace, bro.

If They Think You're Human, Ask for Steak

Dear Gabby,

I think I've found the mother lode. After coming close to getting the sleepy juice at the shelter, I was adopted by a childless couple in the suburbs. Big house, yard, the whole deal. I'm a middle-aged Lhasa apso female; my previous owner was a tough dude living in a small apartment downtown, so to me, this is heaven.

Gabby, they let me sleep with them. I get to eat off of my own plate at the dinner table. They encourage me to beg. I get massages, and home-baked dog cookies. Yesterday I got a cheese enchilada for lunch. I'm not even kidding.

Gabby, do you think I'm being set up? Are they fattening me up for some kind of ritual sacrifice? I mean, they don't even get mad at me when I growl or bite guests; they just explain that I've had a hard life, and then kiss me on the mouth. Truthfully, it's a little sickening, but who am I to complain?

Should I just go along with this, or is the hammer going to fall soon? Any guidance would be greatly appreciated.

Your bud,

Indulged in Indianapolis

DEAR INDULGED,

My heart bleeds for you. Seriously, what a deal! After the hard life you've led, I bet you think you've died and gone to hydrant heaven. Well, it may seem heavenly now, but my instincts tell me you're headed for trouble. I'll explain.

In my earlier letter, "When Your Owner Is a Wimp," Misunderstood went from a similar household into a more regimented family situation, where a dog is a dog and not a human toddler. Oddly enough, it's probably the best thing that could have happened to him, because the change from overindulgence to a more rigid, dog-oriented social situation will ultimately teach him to accept his lowered status in the "pack," preventing aggression and other disruptive behaviors.

In your case, you are being mercilessly spoiled by a childless couple, who sees you as the baby they do not yet have. They have means, a big, comfy home, and lots of displaced love to give. Without a child, they have chosen to give it to you.

Big mistake. Dogs are not people. When a dog is spoiled, especially one from the bad part of town—like you, it immediately surmises that it is darned important, and dominant. They are doing everything wrong. Everything.

I've seen this phenomenon before: The pet becomes a surrogate child, and gets treated as such. Problem is, the dog becomes nearly impossible to deal with, especially when around other people. You're already biting people, a sign that you think you are the head honcho, the "Alpha" whose job it is to discipline anyone who goes against your "dictates."

Listen, pal. Sooner or later, you are going to badly bite a kid or a neighbor, or even one of your owners. When that happens, it's the clink for you, and maybe some of that "sleepy juice." And you know what? It's your mamby-pamby owners' fault. You are NOT a human child, but a dog, with dog instincts. When treated like a king, you automatically develop an inflated opinion of yourself. You rise to the top of the pack, and think you have the right to discipline anyone who doesn't respect your perception of the pack order (however demented that perception is).

In order to prevent your ultimate demise, your owners need to get real, and stop spoiling the crud out of you. Here's what needs to be done:

- You need to be kept out of their bed.
- They need to stop feeding you from the darned table.
- You and your owners need to attend an obedience class—yesterday.
- You cannot receive praise or treats without first earning them.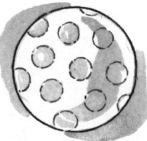
- You cannot lie in their laps.
- Any aggression or obnoxious, pushy behavior on your part

needs to be dealt with immediately, by them, either by a time-out in a crate or by correction with a leash and collar.

◆ You need to be taken out and walked in public, to teach you to behave around others.

◆ You have to be fed at prescribed times during the day, with only dog food given, and not human food.

Here's the rub: Being a tough old Lhasa apso, you may actively resist this new attempt to take you down a notch in the pack hierarchy. If you show overt aggression toward your owners during this transition period, they will need to call in the help of an experienced canine behaviorist, trained to deal with cantankerous dudes like you. Your owners can get a referral from your veterinarian.

None of this will work if your spoiling owners don't get a clue and change their ways. If they continue to mentally diaper you, only trouble can result. If you want to see your next birthday, pal, take my advice and get those marshmallows to treat you like a dog, and not a human toddler with four legs and teeth.

When They Take You for Granted

Dear Gabby,

   I have a pretty good family and a nice home, but lately I've been feeling a bit neglected. I'm a good, low-maintenance dog, friendly to everyone. Older labs are usually that way. I'm eight, so I've mellowed out, and hardly ever make a fuss. Because I'm so easy to take care of, I think my owners have begun to ignore me. Used to be, they'd take me out every day for a walk or a session of fetch, but now, a fast pat on the head and dinner is about all I get. I go potty in the yard, so they don't even need to walk me.

   Gabby, it's not that they leave me alone, but that they don't exactly pay attention to me anymore. I feel like a piece of furniture. They are always there for me if I need them, but something's missing. Can you figure this one out?

   Your bro,

   Disenchanted in Darien

DEAR DISENCHANTED,

I hear you, bro. They aren't really abandoning you (like *Abandoned in Albany*, who wrote "All By Myself"), but sort of taking you for granted. You are so well behaved and laid-back that they just accept your presence, and don't engage with you as much. They are on autopilot; they are physically there, but do not relate much to you anymore.

People do this amongst themselves, too, pal. When things are going well, they tend to take each other for granted. No overt trauma translates into little motivation to act, or interact. It's a relationship killer for them, and a depressant for us.

They need to stop taking you for granted. Heck, you're not going to be around forever; they should enjoy you while they can. They provide you with the essentials, but it's the intangibles that make a life well lived, right?

I've written the following list just for them. If they read it, they'll understand how to involve you more in their lives, and not take you for granted:

- Schedule two 5-minute grooming/petting times each day. The physical closeness will help to bring you closer together.
- Work on teaching your dog a new behavior, maybe a fun trick.
- Massage your dog twice per week.

- Take your dog for a walk once each day, into new areas if possible.
- Sit and talk to your dog.
- Exercise your dog according to its abilities.
- Make eye contact with your dog more often.
- Leave a treat or two down for your dog upon leaving the home.
- Get down on the floor and play with your dog once in a while.

If they abide by these suggestions, you should start feeling better soon. Tough being a well-behaved pooch, huh? Hey, maybe you should start breaking things, or peeing in a corner! Just kidding. Good luck, pal. Don't let life pass you by!

DEAR GABBY'S FAREWELL ADVICE ON "HOW TO THINK LIKE A DOG"

If you've read through all of the fifty letters, you've learned a lot, not only about owners, but about yourselves, and other dogs. I hope I've been able to help out all of you, and that your people will get to browse through the entries and educate themselves a bit. Just think of it: an owner who speaks dog! Actually, that might not be such a great idea . . . we'd probably never get them to shut up. In any event, don't forget to leave this book in the "reading room," where they'll have good access to it.

In this last section, I'd like to give some closing advice on how to get your owner to start thinking like a dog. These ten easy-to-digest mandates summarize the most important things your lovable "two-foots" can do to make life perfect for all you fur balls out there. So, without further ado, let's get to them!

One: *Respect the Pack*

Nothing is more important than the pack. We know that, but sometimes they don't. Be sure your owners can identify the pack hierarchy in your home, especially if there are numerous dogs present. Above all, no dog should be above any person in the pecking order (sorry, pooches). By ensuring this, stability and harmony will be much easier to maintain. No dog should be punished for disciplining a subordinate pet, unless actual injury is imminent. Let them work it out for themselves, people!

Also, realize that owners can minimize most canine leadership problems simply by doing these things:

- ◆ Never spoiling
- ◆ Not allowing their dogs to sleep with them
- ◆ Initiating interactions, instead of letting their dogs do so
- ◆ Not letting their dogs pull on the leash
- ◆ Making sure to teach their dogs basic obedience skills early on
- ◆ Immediately rewarding good behaviors, while discouraging bad
- ◆ Protecting their dogs, while maintaining a confident attitude
- ◆ Building their dogs' confidence with positive reinforcement

- ◆ Never asking their dogs to do something more than once
- ◆ Feeding their dog after they eat

By sticking to these basic principles, an owner should be able to firmly establish him- or herself as the boss of the hacienda. Don't worry, dogs, it's all for the best!

Two: *New Behaviors*
Owners should always strive to teach their dogs as many new behaviors as possible, to feed their curious minds and direct their canine instincts. Tricks or obedience training are fine, as long as the pooch's brain gets a workout!

Three: *Be Consistent*
An owner should always be as consistent as possible, in all he or she does. If it's not cool for you to jump up on the sofa on Tuesday, it shouldn't be okay to do it on a Thursday. Owner inconsistency breeds misbehavior and stress, so don't stand for it!

Four: *Be Fair!*
Nothing is worse than an owner who unfairly punishes a dog, or one who uses a punishment too severe for the transgression. If a dog threatens a child or pees on a guest, by all means, its owner should read it the riot act. But if it sits too slowly or doesn't come as quickly as desired, easy does it! The punishment should always fit the crime.

Five: *Make 'Em Earn it!*
All praise or treats that a dog receives should be in return for services rendered. Owners shouldn't just give a dog a cookie for no reason. Instead, they should ask it to sit or lie down, or at least pay attention for a moment before the reward. Doing so will increase its focus, teach it to think, and convince it that the owner is the boss.

Six: *Safety First*
A dog's environment should be free from any physical dangers, and as stress-free as possible. All potentially dangerous toxins (chemicals, medications, plants, etc.) should be removed from the home, as should any hazardous situations, such as exposed wiring, open windows and doors, or holes in a fence. Other pets or animals that pose a health risk to a dog should be prevented access. Time spent in a vehicle should be limited, and windows should always be cracked!

Seven: *An Interesting Environment*
Owners should respect the fact that dogs are intelligent creatures with insatiable curiosities about their environments. By making a dog's life as interesting and diverse as possible, its owner takes a big step toward preventing mishaps, especially destructive or antisocial behavior. Owners should provide companionship, toys, and chews, and get their dogs out amongst the public!

Eight: *Exercise!*

Dogs are physical creatures, bred to be active. Get your owner to exercise you as often as possible to help you stay in shape, and feel happy and confident. The sedentary dog gets fat, stressed, and troublesome. Avoid this by running, swimming, jumping, and playing!

Nine: *Health*

Your health must be maintained in order for you to be happy and well behaved. Getting you to the veterinarian at least once a year is a vital responsibility of your owner, as is feeding you a quality food, and keeping you well groomed. If he or she does so, you will live a long life, and be the model pooch.

Ten: *Love Your Dog/Love Your Owner!*

Simple, right? It's all you need!

ABOUT THE AUTHOR

The voice of "Dear Gabby" and of his many fans who write in belongs to well-known and highly qualified pet behaviorist **Steve Duno**. Author of nine pet care books that have won him appearances on television and radio, Duno has tackled a wide variety of subject matter, including breed profiling, obedience training, pet health care, solutions to problem behaviors, and even trick training for both dogs and cats. A native New Yorker, he currently lives in Seattle with his well-mannered and lovable thirteen-year-old mutt, Louie, and Flavio, a goofy two-year-old shepherd mix.